The ZEN Ox-H

Zensho W. Kopp

The ZEN Ox-Herding Pictures

Following the Path to Enlightenment

First edition March 2018

All rights reserved. This book, or parts thereof, may not be reproduced in any form without permission.

Translated by John Kitching
Original German title: "Die ZEN-Oschsenbilder – Der Pfad zur Erleuchtung," published 2020 by Synergia, Germany
Ox-herding images: Gyokusei Jikihara Sensei
Cover design: Jörg Zimmermann
Photo back cover: Axel Jung
Back cover quote: ©Zen no bokugyuzu, Sogensha Japan, 1975
Typesetting: John Kitching, Torsten Zander
ISBN 978-3-7534-2149-0
Herstellung und Verlag:
BoD - Books on Demand, Norderstedt

Content

Preface 7

Acknowledgment 9

Introduction 11

I. Seeking the Ox 21

II. Discovering the Tracks 37

III. Finding the Ox 57

IV. Harnessing the Ox 73

V. Taming the Ox 91

VI. Returning home on the Ox's back 103

VII. The Ox is forgotten 115

VIII. Ox and Herder are forgotten 137

XI. Having returned to the Origin 149

X. Entering the market with open hands ... 163

Glossary 177

Contact 207

Preface

This fundamental work of Zen Buddhism is the collective, inspired work of two great Zen masters of the twelfth and twenty-first centuries and of one of the most famous Japanese Zen painters of our times.

The Zen poems and annotations of the Chinese Zen Master Kakuan Shien form the fundamental work, which, without the illuminating commentaries of an equally enlightened Zen master of the present, would be hard to understand. The reason here lies in the extremely profound, symbol-rich language of Kakuan's wonderful poetic verses and likewise of his annotations.

Over time, here in the west, the ten ox-spictures of Zen have appeared in many books. Yet none of them has been able to grasp the deep meaning of the work and bring it to its full expression. The main reason for this lacking lies in the fact that an unenlightened consciousness is never able to expound the Zen way to Enlightenment without first having achieved Enlightenment itself.

Therefore, we the editors consider ourselves fortunate that Zen Master Zensho has now created a new transcription of this very important handbook, to which he has added extensive annotations. Zensho's annotations are an expression of his enlightened consciousness. They are often of provoking, instant directness; they are, very clear, easy to understand and true-to-life.

Zensho's annotations provide the reader with a clear path to a deep understanding of the mysterious truth of the ten ox-herding pictures of Zen.

Without these extremely valuable explanations by one of the Zen masters of our present times, who draws from the same realised dimension of consciousness as Zen Master Kakuan from the twelfth century, the deeper meaning of this exceptional work of Zen literature would remain concealed from us.

Zensho's annotations, in which the old Chinese masters have their say too, are very practical and a unique orientation aid and an inexhaustible source of inspiration.

The reader will make best use of this book when he repeatedly pauses and allows what he has read to take effect. The profundity of the sayings in this book thus becomes increasingly clear through repeated reading and all the more so when put into practice.
May this book help all those who read it to realise their immortal, true self.

The Editors
Zen Center Tao Chan
Wiesbaden Germany, March 2018

Acknowledgments

The ox-herding paintings in this book, created in tusche by the Japanese painter Gyokusei Jikihara Sensei are impressive examples of Nanga brush painting in the traditional Chinese style. The editors and Zen Master Zensho would like to thank the staff at the Zen Mountain Monastery, Mount Tremper, New York for their kind permission to print these images, which through this book, are now available to a wider public.

禅

Zen

Introduction

This modern handbook of Zen is a classic of Zen literature and belongs to the fundamental, essential texts of Zen Buddhism. It is an extremely valuable guide on the path to Enlightenment and a limitless source of the mystical wisdom of Zen.

Of all representations of the various levels of spiritual realisation on the path of Zen, none is as profound and at the same time as fascinating as the ten ox-herding pictures of Zen. The Japanese Zen Master Zenkei Shibayama (twentieth century) says:

> Since the beginning of Zen Buddhism there has been a whole series of writings to explain the practice methods and teachings of Zen.
> Yet there has been no book which has portrayed them so clearly and distinctly as the "Ten Ox-Herding Pictures of Zen". They explain it completely and unveil the profound truth of Zen.

The symbolic representation of the Zen path to Enlightenment by means of the pictorial story of a herder, searching for his lost ox – his true self, originates from the golden age of ancient China.

The original version of the picture-cycle, which was firstly made up of six and later eight pictures, was painted by Buddhist teachers of Soto-Zen, who held the view that Enlightenment is a gradual on-going process.

All these representations had tried in the same manner to depict the on-going process of Zen training using a black ox which became increasing white from picture to picture. Here, the colour black portrayed the tainted mind, tarnished by spiritual blindness.

However, in the twelfth century, the Chinese Zen Master Kakuan Shien produced a version with ten ox paintings and added an annotation to each one. Kakuan lived and taught at the Liang-shan Zen temple in Tingdschou, China. He was the spiritual heir to Zen Master Tai-sui Yüan-ching from the Lin-chi line of tradition and belonged to the twelfth generation following Lin-chi.

As opposed to earlier representations, Kakuan's ox-herding pictures show an ox that does not become progressively white – his ox remains unchangingly black throughout the pictures. In this way, he clearly expresses that, in truth, the original mind was never tarnished since it is eternally pure and unchanging. Through this, Kakuan rises above the old, limited viewpoint of earlier ox-book authors and proclaims:

> The radiating light of the One Mind has been shining since timeless eternity and nothing can obscure it.

This is the essential core idea which interweaves Kakuan's brilliant work "The Ten Ox-Herding Pictures of Zen" like a golden thread.

However, this does not mean that there is no development process of spiritual maturing in Kakuan's Ten Ox-herding Pictures. For his Zen is the southern, dynamic Lin-chi Zen of immediate perception by becoming aware of the mind – right up to complete awakening in the realisation of sudden Enlightenment.

This version of Zen Master Kakuan's Ten Ox-herding Pictures of Zen found its farthest widespread adoption in Japan following the Ashikaga-period as a never-ending source of profound wisdom of Zen and a steadfast spiritual guide. It was considered an essential Zen text of unique value and renowned as the most important ox-herding book.

Although Kakuan's ox-herding pictures, which once set an example for many painters, have become lost over time, his wonderful poems of highest expressive force fortunately remain for us, as well as his accompanying comments. These texts, together with the inspired ink paintings by the Japanese Zen painter Gyokusei Jikihara Sensei (1904-2005), form the basis of this book.

Jikihara Sensei was a highly esteemed contemporary painter in Japan and practised Zen under Zen Master Zenkei Shibayama. His ox-herding paintings in this book, painted in tusche, are unique examples of Nanga brush painting in the traditional Chinese style. The paintings, which breathe the spirit of Zen, are an expression of his expert mastery of tusche painting and stand out by the uniqueness of his brushwork.

Yet what prompted Zen Master Kakuan to add two new pictures to the eight which existed in the original version of the twelfth century and thus create a version of ten pictures? The ox-herding picture series of earlier authors, which existed up to that time, ended with the eighth picture, the empty circle "Enso" – in Zen the symbol of Enlightenment – as if, with this, the Zen path would thus be at an end.

However, Kakuan, as a true, fully realised Zen Master goes beyond this limited notion of Enlightenment with the two, extremely meaningful pictures he includes. His version is pure, living Zen and goes much further and deeper than previous depictions which ended with the eighth picture. Thus we see on his ninth picture a wonderful nature idyll as a pointer to the fact that the enlightened one, in his realisation of the non-discriminating clarity of the mind, lives in the all-embracing wholeness of being. In the words of Kakuan:

> He has returned to the origin.
> He beholds the alternating coming and going of all life in the world and abides in serene non-action.

By awakening from the dream of birth and death he has risen above all duality, and thus the whole world transforms itself for him into the great revelation of transcendental wisdom. Without exception, he now experiences all that exists as the timeless reality of the One Mind, and when he acts, everything he does is the wonderful act of Buddha.

In the tenth, final ox-herding picture we see how the enlightened one enters the marketplace in the world with a broad laugh covering his entire face. In his utter realisation of Enlightenment he moves among the crowd in great compassion and total freedom in order to liberate them from the ignorance which causes them suffering, so that they awaken to their true self. Kakuan says:

> He shows bar-keepers and fishmongers the way of awakening to their true self.

Zen is the way of "sudden Enlightenment". It is the essential feature of the Zen of the old, great Chinese masters like Hui-neng, Ma-tsu or Lin-chi when compared to all the other teachings in Buddhism. However, we should make it clear to ourselves that sudden Enlightenment does not just happen by chance, unexpectedly and just like that, without any spiritual preparation.

Instead, the term "sudden Enlightenment" means that the true, direct Zen way to liberation is not made up of predefined, dogmatic fixed steps, unlike most Buddhist schools. For clinging to predefined steps suppresses and even prevents the creative ability for an intuitive, direct understanding and limits the free mind.

Consequently, we should also not make the mistake of interpreting the systematic order of Kakuan's ox-herding pictures as a way by steps to Enlightenment. For this would not be in keeping with the true, free mind of Zen and is indeed diametrically opposed to it. However, we are not in conflict with the principle of Zen of sudden Enlightenment when we speak of an ongoing spiritual process of maturing.

Thus, the Zen way of awakening to our true self in terms of the ten ox-herding pictures features different levels of spiritual realisation, even when Enlightenment itself happens very suddenly, in an instant, following a long process of spiritual maturing.

In an instant, in a single, blessed moment, the mind expands into boundlessness and a new perspective opens to us which transforms our whole essence.

Thus Kakuan's ten ox-herding pictures of Zen in this book show us the "Zen way of sudden Enlightenment through spiritual realisation".

Spring 2018   Zensho W. Kopp

禅
道

Zen Path

The ZEN Ox-Herding Pictures of Zen

The mind-ox is our original, innermost essence. Its bright gleam of clear light has been shining since time immemorial.

Zen Master Kakuan Shien

I.

Seeking the Ox

從來不失，今用追尋。

Poem and annotation by Kakuan

Desolate in the endless wilderness of this world, he cleaves his way through the tall grass in search of his ox.
Following nameless rivers, lost on the intertwining paths of mountains afar.
Utterly exhausted, his heart is in despair, he cannot find the ox.
In the evening mist he hears only
the chirping of the cicadas.

In reality, the ox has never become lost. So why seek it? He is only unable to find it because he is separated from his true nature.

His senses confused, he has lost the trail in the dusty distance. Far astray from his homeland he arrives at a bewilderment of paths. Yet which one is correct? Desire for profit and fear of loss break out like a blazing fire, and notions of right and wrong rise up against one another like spearheads on the battlefield.

Comment by Zensho

> Desolate in the endless wilderness of this world, he cleaves his way through the tall grass in search of his ox.

In Zen Buddhism, the ox symbolises the reality of our true essence. Whoever goes in search of his lost ox finds himself on the path to his true self; his immanent buddha-nature. The ten ox-herding pictures illustrate this very impressively by showing the Zen path to liberation from the beginning of the spiritual search right up to complete Enlightenment and the ensuing actions and effect of the enlightened one in the world.

In all that exists and in all life, the radiating light of the One Mind shines as the reality of our true self. There is only one sole essence, the One Mind, beside which nothing else exists. It is the sole reality at the deepest base of all living beings and things.

We are all living in direct unity with this, our true essence – nothing could be closer. As the reality existing of its own, it is constantly present in the innermost ground of each and every person. It is that universal, eternal truth of which the great, enlightened masters of all religions have proclaimed for thousands of years, in which a person awakens from his dream of birth and death and experiences his true, birthless, undying self.

Yet generally speaking, people are convinced that their life began with their birth and will end with their death. However, this is a huge, fateful mistake for it only pertains to our physical body. The truth of Zen is that there is a true self, which is the eternal, timeless reality of our true essence and was not born and will never die.

Our birth is not the beginning of our life since our true essence precedes our birth, and this means – we are life. And if our true essence is already there before our birth, it will also be there after our death. Recognising this – our original, undying essential-nature – is the true meaning of our life and thus the most important goal of our human existence. Therefore, becoming aware of and awakening to our birth- and deathless true self is life's highest experience.

Whatever you may achieve in your life, be it riches, esteem or power, there always remains a feeling of inadequacy and the discontent that comes with it. All these things cannot really satisfy you and they do not correspond to your real, fundamental need since in truth, you are yearning for something completely different. Yet that which you yearn for and seek, without really knowing what you are actually seeking, cannot be found externally, however much you may try.

You can find it nowhere other than within yourself, for it is your true destiny to experience your innermost essential-ground within yourself. It is constantly present, without you knowing it. Therefore it is written in Zen Master Kakuan's commentary on the first ox-herding picture:

> *In reality, the ox has never become lost. So why seek it?*
> *Due only to the separation from his true nature is he unable to find it.*

An old Zen-saying goes: "Where will you seek your ox when you are already sitting on the ox you are seeking?" Your deepest mind-essence is given by nature and does not originally belong to the realm of realisation. So how could it become lost? You have lost your mind-ox in the tall grass, the creeping tangle of your spiritual blindness, solely because you have turned away from the reality of your true being. The following example shows us this too:

> A Zen monk comes to the Chinese Zen Master Joshu (ninth century) and asks him:

> "What is the meaning of 'our great teacher Bodhidharma (sixth century), the first patriarch of Zen came from the West'?"
> Joshu answers: "A cow has broken out of the stall."

The Ten Ox-Herding Pictures of Zen are based exactly on this one situation where the cow, that is, the mind-ox, has broken out of the stall of your spiritual awareness. And now you must once again find your mind-ox – your true self.

Who am I? What is my true self? What is the true purpose of life? What happens to me when I die? These questions have the same meaning as 'the search for the mind-ox', it is the search for the reality of your true self.

If you do not find an answer to this essential question in the sense of an understanding that lights up your whole being, you have completely missed the point of your whole life. For as long as you do not know who and what you are in the depths of your being, all your actions and aspirations are completely meaningless, regardless of what you achieve since you have passed by the true meaning of life.

> *His senses confused, he has lost the trail in the dusty distance.*

By externalizing your senses you live your life in mindless routine and indifferent ignorance, missing out on the essential and losing yourself in the trivialities of daily life. Yet it is of the utmost urgency that right "now", without hesitation, you begin the search for the mind-ox, your true self. Otherwise, your death will be just the pitiful conclusion of a senselessly wasted life. Thus, the Chinese Zen Master Jung-chia (eighth century) speaks the admonishing words:

> The matter of life and death is immense and impermanence grasps hold in a flash. How can you waste your time with trivialities?

Yet regrettably, most people are completely unreceptive to this undeniable fact, so that they lack an insight into the necessity of a spiritual change. If, however, in your present life, you find a good spiritual teacher through the effect of your positive karma or you even encounter an enlightened master who guides you, such that you become aware of your true self, it is a great blessing.

In this recollection of your true, divine nature, which you have forgotten, the desire for liberation grows within you since you have understood that the essence is missing. You have lost yourself and you no longer know who and what you really are.

This is the situation in the first ox-herding picture, in which the herder sets out to once again find his lost mind-ox – his true self. Yet where should he seek? His senses confused, he has lost the trail of the ox in the dusty distance of his spiritual blindness and he does not know the way. Kakuan says of this:

Far astray from his homeland he arrives at a bewilderment of paths. Yet which one is correct?

"Which path is the correct one?" asks Zen Master Kakuan in his commentary on the poem. Yet how can you know which way is correct as long as you have not yet reached spiritual clarity?

Following nameless rivers, lost on the intertwining paths of mountains afar. Utterly exhausted, his heart is in despair, he cannot find the ox.

The search for the mind-ox, your true self, proves to be difficult for you because the truth you are seeking is not only unknown but also unnameable and thus "nameless".

If you nonetheless follow the concepts of predefined teachings, you follow the seemingly certain path of the rivers "with" names. Yet how can it be possible for you to find your mind-ox as your uttermost, true self when you follow the intertwining paths of dogmatic speculation, lost is the mountains of unyielding concepts?

Whichever religion or philosophy you may turn to, at some point on your spiritual transformation process to liberation you must free yourself again from the choking fetters of a predefined doctrine. For ultimately, the path of Zen is all about achieving a direct perception of that which is constantly present within us and all around us as our utmost innate true being. "That there is nothing to achieve are not empty words but the highest truth", says the Chinese Zen Master Huang-po (ninth century). There is no doctrine to study. This is an essential prerequisite for an understanding of Zen.

However, when you lose yourself in the labyrinth of Buddhist erudition and only seek outwardly, you have turned away from your own mind-ox. You have turned away from the truth of Zen and have become lost in the evening mists of your spiritual darkness. To this, the Chinese Zen Master Lin-chi (ninth century) says:

> You cling to names and sayings, and these turn to obstacles and conceal your perception of the truth. Yet simply allow your

discriminating thinking and seeking to come to rest. Trust in that which acts within you in this instant, and there is nothing more to seek.

Behind every answer you have found by means of discriminating, conceptual thought, a new question arises, so that the more you strive to reach your goal, the more you veer away from it. In the Shodoka Zen text, the "Song of the Realization of the Way" by the Chinese Zen Master Yung-chia from the eighth century there is the following saying:

> Directly cutting out the root,
> that is the Buddha-seal.
> I do not care for collecting leaves and searching for twigs.

The highest truth cannot be expressed in words since it is beyond everything that sense and reason can comprehend. Each attempt, however well-meant it may be, to describe the inexpressible truth within the bounds of our limited human speech is like trying to capture heaven in a net and is completely pointless, bringing only confusion.

Nonetheless, most people cling tightly to their conditioned notions and only act within their self-created boundaries. The result is that they deem false whatever transcends their limited imagination. In this way, they constantly project an accumulation of dark clouds of discriminating, conceptual thinking that obscure the boundless expanse of the Mind and thus their own divine being.

> Desire for profit and fear of loss break out like a blazing fire, and notions of right and wrong rise up against one another like spearheads on the battlefield.

When you are caught up like this in the creeping tangle of discriminating, conceptual thinking, you are just living elsewhere and are missing out on the essential – the present moment. If your consciousness abides in the past or the future, you miss out on the constant presence of divine being in the absolute present of Now. For divine reality "is" timeless Now.

> **In the evening mist he hears but the chirping of the cicadas.**

Zen practice is about making efforts to liberate yourself from the shadow of habitual, conditioned thinking and the constantly flowing current of thoughts, like the cicadas, chirping in your consciousness.

In this ongoing process of your spiritual clarity you likewise become able to suspend each habitual act of attaching to something. True Zen practice is to place all your effort in concentrating on this goal with your whole being. The highest truth is beyond all words, concepts, notions and beyond all attaching and rejecting. Hence, the Chinese Zen Master Pao-chi (ninth century) says:

> External knowledge is nothing other than ignorance. So why seek externally for a treasure when your innermost essence holds its own radiating jewel? Ultimately, all external seeking is empty and void, and only leads to mental exhaustion. Therefore, seek nothing other than the clear, empty space of the mind. There is not one single thing for you to gain.

"There is nothing to seek since there is nothing to gain!" This is the fundamental truth of Zen. There is no space in which things could be separate from one another, and there is no time in which anything is yet to appear or is no longer there. For everything takes place simultaneously, whereby all things mutually permeate one another. What prevents you from perceiving your mind-ox – your original true nature – is nothing other than the power of habitual, dualistic deception. Yet if your mind were to be completely free from all attaching and rejecting, how could deceptions and conditioned notions then arise? Your subjective discrimination, the constant grasping and rejecting, robs you of your spiritual independence and allow you to fall prey to the hypnotic influence of things. All this must go. Then you will witness that the mind-ox you seek is constantly present in its entire magnificence because it has always been present. It was always there but "you" were not there.

Wherever you may be, the all-embracing reality of your true being is constantly present within you and around you. You cannot evade the mind-ox, neither in the silence of a beautiful, idyllic countryside nor in the midst of the hustle and bustle of the world. For this reason, in the eighth century the sixth patriarch of Zen, Zen Master Hui-neng said: "Everywhere, even in the midst of worldly passions and erroneous opinions there dwells the unborn, primordial true self."

Everything, whatever and wherever it may be, holds within it the mind-ox, your unborn, eternal buddha-nature. But in your spiritual blindness you are blind to reality and so you seek your true self outside of yourself.

Zen practice in the sense of the "Ten Ox-Herding Pictures" thus consists of moving your mental perspective from seeking externally to seeking within, and of rediscovering your lost mind-ox within yourself. Yet since this discovery is beyond all intellectual understanding, as the truth that transcends all comprehension, it must become your own real experience.

However, this requires serious spiritual instruction under the leadership of a true master on your spiritual path and an unwavering great trust in the original purity of your own mind. The master knows and shows you the way that leads you to your lost ox. Ultimately, your resolute, full commitment is essential for you to once again find your mind-ox. Although the master shows you the way, you must nonetheless go it yourself.

When you genuinely endeavour in this way to find the truth beyond all words, you will also find the ox's tracks in your continual perseverance in the practice of Zen.

II.

Discovering the Tracks

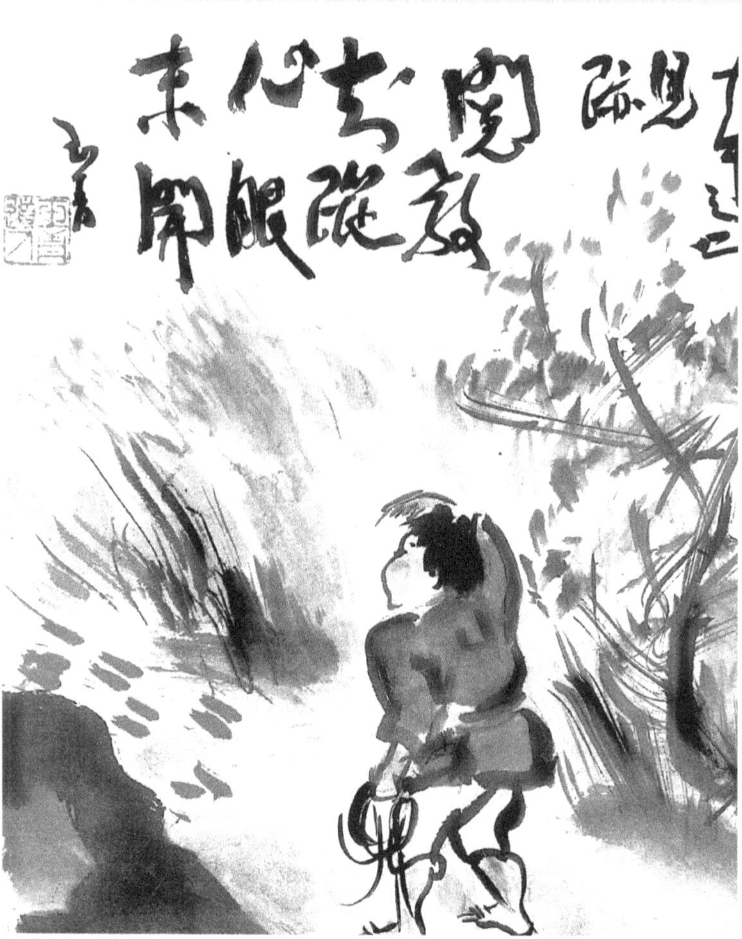

Poem and annotation by Kakuan

Beside the river, under the trees, he discovers the ox's tracks! Even amid the fragrant grass he sees its trail.
No matter how far the ox may go, even as far as into the deepest canyons of remote mountains, the trail can no more be hidden than one's own nose, looking heavenward.

Through his understand of the teachings, he finds the ox's footsteps. He now understands that all things, however diverse they may appear, are of the same gold, and that everything that exists is no different from his own essence.
However, he cannot yet distinguish the true from the untrue. He has yet to pass through the gate but he has recognised the path.

Comment by Zensho

> Beside the river, under the trees, he discovers the ox's tracks! Even amid the fragrant grass he sees its trail.

When you seriously apply yourself to the teachings of Zen it will become clear to you that the truth can only be found beyond all words, and not in words or letters. Through your Zen practice you have now reached a certain understanding of the teachings – you have found the ox's tracks.

> Through his understand of the teachings he finds the ox's footsteps.

Yet no matter how far your initial, intellectual understanding may go, it is never enough to perceive the profound truth of Zen. For however valuable all the spiritual explanations by the enlightened masters, the sutras and the teachings may be, they are only the footsteps of the ox but not the mind-ox itself.

Indeed, the mind-ox will only reveal itself to you when you have transcended all theoretic teachings and have reached the essence. As long as you still place your trust in external teachings and borrowed beliefs, you are still very far away from the reality of your true being. You are bound by the concepts of the delusion of discriminating, conceptual thinking and have limited yourself. To this, the following encounter:

> A monk asks Zen Master Yuan-wu (twelfth century): "What is the fundamental truth of the holy teachings?" Yuan-wu replies, "A post, to which to tie a donkey."

Question all religious and philosophical belief systems! In the eyes of Zen, they are nothing more than mind-bending speculations and interpretations of the neurotic mind. You do not need to believe in any religious dogma, for dogmas are no more than bonds for the free mind and an obstacle on the path to liberation. Just like Buddhist rules and rites, in the eyes of the old Chinese Zen masters, dogmas are just obstructing residues of dualistic thinking.

With the greatest of emphasis, the old Chinese Zen masters constantly pointed to the fact that in Zen, there is nothing to learn and nothing to achieve. Thus, they taught nothing other than the "Buddha-Dharma", the Buddha-law – the truth of the One Mind, beside which nothing else exists. In Zen, as opposed to conventional, customary Buddhism,

Buddha-Dharma does not refer to any teaching that can be conveyed in words but instead, it refers to the highest truth, inaccessible to discriminating, conceptual thinking.

It is that essential truth which led to Buddha's teachings and can only be grasped in a direct, intuitive understanding in the experience of Enlightenment – Satori.

For this reason, the Zen masters constantly point directly to a person's Heart-Mind so that he perceives his true self and achieves Buddhahood. The Chinese Zen Master Fen-yang (eleventh century) says of this:

> When you are blinded and full of doubt, a thousand holy scriptures will not even help you. Yet when you have achieved an understanding, then even one word is too much. Zen is transmitted personally by recognising the Heart-Mind. It is not passed on externally through written words.

To search for the truth, as the reality of our true being, externally and view it as something different from ourselves corresponds to the dualistic way of thinking of intellectual interpretation. Yet since we are already in the midst of this truth and live through this truth, we cannot be different or separated from it. Hence, the Chinese Zen Master Ta-hui (twelfth century) says:

> The realm of Enlightenment is no external realm with visible characteristics. Buddhahood is the realm of highest knowledge, which you can only find within yourself.

Here, the path of Zen Buddhism differs radically from all other religious systems and philosophical teachings. For Zen is a matter of pure experiencing in absolute directness. This is expressed in the summary of the four fundamental tenets of Zen from the early Tang-dynasty in China:

1. Transmission outside orthodox teaching
2. Independence from sacred texts
3. Directly pointing to the Heart-Mind
4. Perceiving one's own nature and achieving Buddhahood

Zen has but one concern. It wishes to thoroughly destroy all your attachments to words and notions, in whatever form they may be, so that you awaken from the dream of birth and death. However, we must not make the mistake from the outset of avoiding to read the fundamental and essential texts that are required for an understanding of the truth of Zen. For surely, without at least an initial understanding of the theoretical foundations we will hardly understand what the practice of Zen is actually about.

Just as one must pass from the shallow to the deep, an examination of the essential Zen texts is of great value for those who earnestly practise on the Zen path. Yet it is a fatal mistake if you believe that this is enough, since you will just stand still.

The sayings of the old Chinese Zen masters are great, they are wonderful, brilliant. Their enlightened words bear witness to the profound truth of Zen and are of immeasurable value. However, whilst reading, you must not forget that the truth you are seeking in the texts of the old masters is nothing other than your very own true essence.

You are seeking something which in reality you yourself are – even though, tragically you have forgotten it, and no longer know who or what you are in your deepest essence. That is why all buddhas and patriarchs, all the great masters of Zen, constantly point to nothing other than a person's "Heart-Mind", in order for you to perceive your birth- and deathless true self and achieve Buddhahood.

Sadly, people, in their spiritual blindness, cannot and do not want to believe that the own mind is the consummate buddha, and thus, in their spiritual unknowing, they cling to external teachings and seek the truth outside of themselves.

Yet you will only know what the truth is when you immediately immerse yourself, diving directly into the ocean of wisdom, into the boundless ocean of the One Mind. Do you want to know how an apple tastes? Then take a bite of it and you will know. Do you want to know how water is? Then drink it – or dive into it! This is the way of Zen.

Many words confuse the mind, yet where words are silent, the Eternal begins. All thinking is an erroneous belief and whatever results from it is just empty concepts. Yet behind this lies eternity, which lights up the entire universe with its radiating light.

This enlightening self-mind is an all-embracing whole which contains everything within it in a wonderful way. This instant, right here where you are, it reveals itself as the reality you are seeking. This reality of your true being reveals itself "now-here", it lies neither in the past nor in the future. For the past has already happened, and the future does not yet exist.

Past and future are nothing other than thoughts that appear in the mind at the present moment. Hence, the experience of time is nothing more than thought. Yet "all thought is an erroneous belief", as

Zen puts it, and so time is non-existent. The Chinese Zen Master Huang-po (ninth century), one of the greatest masters in the history of Zen, expresses this as follows:

> As soon as thoughts arise you succumb to dualism. Time without beginning and the present moment are one and the same. There is no beforehand and no afterwards. Due only to your ignorance do you discriminate between these two. If you would understand, however, how could there be any discrimination?

"Now" is timeless eternity itself, and space and time are nothing other than the result of thinking and therefore illusion. It is of vital importance that you make it clear to yourself that the truth you are seeking is constantly present now-here as your very own true self. For this reason we read in the text of the first ox-herding picture:

> In reality, the ox has never become lost. So why seek it?

Thus, true seeking in the spirit of Zen is "learning that there is nothing to learn and nothing to seek". For where nothing is sought, the unborn mind is present. It is also constantly present whilst you are seeking it. Yet precisely due to your seeking and brooding, you cover this radiating splendour of your true self with the dark clouds of your discriminating ignorance.

> A monk asked Zen Master Joshu, "The white cow in the distant field – where is it?"
> Joshu replied, "Under the moonlight there is no need for colour."
> The monk asked, "So what does the cow live on?"
> Joshu, "It never chews around on anything."
> The monk pleads, "Master, please answer."
> Joshu said, "This is simply the way I am."

The radiating splendour of the One Mind is omnipresent and thus, there is nothing to achieve. This is the absolute truth. You really need not do anything apart from immersing yourself in what you are at the base of your being.

Following the path of Zen means completely immersing yourself with your whole being in the immediateness of here and now – everywhere and all the time, wherever you are and whatever you are doing. For since reality is the all-embracing wholeness of being, it encompasses empty, boundless space and the three time-forms: past, present and future in a single Now.

The fullness of divine being is constantly present and reveals itself now-here, in this moment, right there where you are. If you miss out on the present moment, you live in the illusion of time and miss out on true life. For life does not happen yesterday or tomorrow but always in the present moment of "now". The following Mondo illustrates this:

> A Zen novice came to the Chinese Zen Master Nansen (ninth century) and said, "Master, I am new at the monastery and I seek the way to Enlightenment. Please advise me how to find it."
>
> Master Nansen asked, "Do you hear the rushing of the river? If you do then that is the way."

So be truly "here" with your whole being "now", this instant! Open yourself completely to the immediate presence of being! This is the instantaneous way to directly perceiving reality as it is.

Zen is the radical path of direct, immediate perception, without the frills. It does not provide any erudite, verbose explanation and does not make use of any cumbersome circumlocutions and generalisations. For no explanation, no matter how verbose it may be, will bring those seeking liberation any closer to their true self. This original, direct and spontaneous teaching method unhinges the intellect and short circuits the thoughts.

> One day, a Zen monk came to Zen Master Joshu and asked him, "Which Zen was once brought from India to China by the first patriarch Bodhidharma?"
> Joshu answered, "What sense is there in speaking of such an old story? What is 'your' Zen 'now' at this very moment?"

Zen constantly refers to the direct experience of pure truth and points with tremendous emphasis to your own heart, without becoming caught in the tangle of thoughts and concepts. The principal characteristic of Zen is undoubtedly its incomprehensibility. Just like water flowing through your fingers it evades all definition. Things are completely clear but they become unclear due to your discriminating, conceptual thinking, and the mind-ox you seek moves further and further away. That is why a Zen master sees it as his special duty to liberate his student from the prison of his intellect so that the inner eye of wisdom opens to him.

> A very well-read Buddhist asks Zen Master Lin-chi, "Is it indeed so that the three Buddhist schools explain the twelvefold teaching and Buddha's essence?"
>
> Lin-chi says, "Have you not yet pulled up your weeds?"

Zen can never be made the object of logical deliberations and explanations. Instead, to really understand its truth, it must be lived within us at our innermost. Therefore, spiritual development towards an intuitive understanding is always essential in Zen, achieved through practice as opposed to intellectual studies..

By reaching this intuitive understanding, as in this second ox-herding picture, you have gained a feeling for the all-embracing wholeness of being through your spiritual transformation to a higher consciousness level.

He now understands that all things, however diverse they may appear, are of the same gold and that everything which exists is no different from his own essence.

The sun, moon, stars and the heavens, the mountains, rivers and all living things have a single, integral essence. All phenomena are a wonderful revelation of the mind-ox. The rushing of a mountain stream and the singing of the birds are the absolute, universal truth, and the silent, green mountain is the body of Buddha. Everything is the One Mind, beside which nothing else exists. Endless and all-pervading, it radiates throughout the entire universe.

Everything, whatever it may be, is the One. All phenomena are a revelation of the one reality and permeate one another completely without any limitations. This truth of the all-embracing wholeness of being, "Hua-yen", is the crown of all Buddhist teachings and likewise a synthesis of all the essential thoughts of Mahayana.

In Hua-yen, the universal One Mind is compared to the boundless surface of an ocean, in which all things and events permeate one another in an all-embracing whole, which contains everything within itself. Everything is in perfect harmony, for everything is the manifestation of a fundamental mind, similar to waves on the ocean. Everything in the universe, whether living or non-living, is thus the One Mind, beside which nothing else exists.

The perceiver, the process of perception and the object of perception – everything is a sole being. "Form is emptiness, and emptiness is form", the Hridaya-Sutra tells us, the "Heart-Sutra of Perfect

Wisdom", which is recited daily in the Zen Buddhist monasteries. Form is emptiness, "Shunyata". Empty means without own-substance, without Being existing of its own. It is just phenomena – just empty form.

> Once, when Zen Master Hui-chung (eighth century) was at the court, the emperor Su-Dsung asked him, "Master, which high insights have you achieved?"
> "Do you see the clouds in the sky, your Majesty?" the master replied.
> "Certainly, I see them," said the emperor.
> "Now I ask you, your Majesty, do you think that the clouds are nailed to the sky or have been hung onto them?"

You cannot nail a board to the void, as it is said in Zen. All things are empty, without substance, there is nothing you can grasp on to. They are like clouds passing in the sky, whose destiny it is to dissipate away again at some point. All the things in our external world of phenomena are nothing other than empty forms. This means they are nothing other than empty.

However, empty does not mean that the world we perceive does not exist, but rather that it is nothing other than pure phenomenon without any reality. In other words, it is not "non-existent" but rather "unreal". These two concepts are entirely different in their meaning and should not be confused with one another.

For example, we cannot even imaging a round triangle, and thus it is "non-existent". On the other hand, a mirage belongs to the things that exist, although it is unreal and thus has no reality whatsoever, which means that it is "unreal". Buddhist understanding of the voidness of all phenomena is therefore no nihilistic standpoint. It is far more about making it clear that all things are empty, since all underlying substantiality is missing.

It is general belief that our mind assimilates external sensory impressions, but this is a great misconception, for everything takes place in your own mind. There are no phenomena that are not in the mind because all things come from out of it, through it and are in it.

If you are genuinely determined to find your lost mind-ox again, it is absolutely necessary to have unwavering trust in the Voidness Doctrine of Buddhism; in the "Mind-Only-Teaching". Therefore, you should give up all your previous knowledge and understanding and view the world as an illusion. Everything you see is just an illusory magical spectacle of the mind, like mirages, empty images – just like the moon reflecting in the water.

Non-perception of this universal truth is seen in Mahayana and Zen Buddhism as the real, root cause of one's being bound to Samsara – the cycle of birth and death. This unknowingness is the root of all suffering since it is that state of mind which does not correspond to reality. So therefore, non-perceiving of the voidness of all things and the deceptive nature of all phenomena is the real cause of all suffering.

However, not only the external world of phenomena but also all habitual thoughts, passions, all mental confusion and feelings are equally without substance, not real and are instead rootless and flowing. Correspondingly, all obstacles on the path to liberation which arise from Karma-created passions are also originally non-existent. For cause and effect are nothing more than a dream, without any reality.

There is no external world of phenomena for you to overcome, neither is there anything like Enlightenment for you to achieve. The reality of your true self and the external world are one and the same. Everything you perceive is just projections of your own mind, like in a dream, and thus the mind itself. Nothing comes from outside of the mind. If you believe you perceive something externally, it only means that it appears in the consciousness.

> No matter how far the ox may go, even as far as into the deepest canyons of remote mountains, the trail can no more be hidden than one's own nose, looking heavenward.

Everything is the One Mind, beside which nothing else exists. Wherever you go, even if you go into the deepest canyons of remote mountains, everything you perceive is the mind-ox, your true essence which you seek. The mind-ox is present everywhere, you cannot escape from it. Yet since in your spiritual blindness you are lacking the correct discernment, Kakuan says in his commentary to the poem:

> *Still, he cannot yet distinguish the true from the untrue. He has yet to pass through the gate but he has recognised the path.*

Even when you have achieved a certain intuitive understanding on the Zen path, your spiritual eye has yet to open. You are still far from having passed through the gate to liberation. Yet you have recognised the path and have discovered the tracks which will lead you to your true self, the lost mind-ox.

III.

Finding the Ox

從牛多父兄家
逐深

十牛圖之三

Poem and annotation by Kakuan

The nightingale's singing echoes lucidly. The sun shines softly, the breeze is mild, the willows by the river are green.
There stands the ox, no longer can anything conceal it.
Yet which artist can paint this majestic head with its magnificent horns?

When you hear the song, you can sense the origin. As soon as the six senses have blown past on the breeze, you have passed through the gate. Wherever you may go you see the ox's head everywhere. This unity is like salt in water and colour in ink. Not even the smallest thing is different from the true self.

Comment by Zensho

The nightingale's singing echoes lucidly.
The sun shines softly, the breeze is mild, the willows by the river are green.

In your transformation to a higher level of consciousness you become more receptive to all that exists. You become more and more awake and aware of the self-revelation of the own mind in all things. You hear the nightingale's song and can sense the origin of the singing as the revelation of divine reality. That is why in Zen Master Kakuan's annotation to the poem it is written:

> *When you hear the song, you can sense the origin. As soon as the six senses have blown past on the breeze, you have passed through the gate. Wherever you may go you see the ox's head everywhere.*

The Chinese Zen Master Hong-zhi (twelfth century) says of this:

> When your perception of objects does not dazzle you, you see that all things are the

light of the mind. With every step, you transcend all boundaries, completely free, dwelling nowhere. You open yourself to the world in great clarity and with a natural, open awareness.

"As soon as the six senses have blown past on the breeze", so that the perception of objects does not dazzle you – what does this mean? You are dazzled when you are confused by the many phenomena of an apparent, external world. When your mind is not influenced by the impressions of the senses, you will not be confused by your perception of an external world of phenomena, and you will realise that all phenomena are the mind itself.

Thus, it is a matter of passing through the midst of the external world of phenomena and retaining self-awareness of mind. You perceive something, view it and at the same time, you abide in spiritual awareness and thus in your centre. Then you can precisely see how the tendency arises in your mind to make reference to what you perceive in the form of attaching and rejecting.

Yet the fact that you just views things without wishing to alter anything means that your thinking cannot take on a life of its own, and you remain at ease in cheerfully relaxed self-awareness. The

Chinese Zen Master Ta-hui (twelfth century) gives us a good description of this active Zen way:

> That high awareness of mind which you have practised in silence so keenly should above all be applied when you are entangled in the external turmoil of daily life. If you find this too difficult it only means that you have not yet achieved enough spiritual awareness from your Zen meditation in silence.
>
> If you are convinced that meditation in silence is better than meditation during your activities, you have fallen into the trap of searching for reality by fleeing from external manifestations and you have misunderstood the cause of your spiritual confusion.
>
> If you are longing for quietude and you loathe the trouble and noise, it is time for you to put all your efforts into action. Suddenly, the fulfilment you have so strenuously achieved in your silent meditation will be bestow upon you in the midst of all the noise.

There is no doubt that this powerful Zen way of active meditation in the midst of the tumultuous world is the surest and fastest way of achieving a constant experience of the all-embracing, all-pervading presence of divine being. Thus, Zen practice is about achieving a perspicuity of consciousness which raises you above each illusion of multiplicity. In this way you will increasingly understand and experience that all things, all phenomena, everything you see and that comes your way is the mind-ox, that is, the One Mind itself, in the form in which it appears before you.

Everything is a great, all-embracing whole which contains everything within itself in a wonderful, perfect way. You look outwards and this, your act of looking outwards is a non-looking-outwards since your perception is no longer viewing things in a dualistic way.

So too in an old Zen saying, it is written: "To hear with the eyes and see with the ears is true understanding." Here, there is no outside and no inside. There is nothing but pure "suchness", Tathata – the empty, true nature of all things. In this state of mind, in which you become aware of the all-embracing wholeness of all being, you reach the ground of Being in a blessed instant of inward-sightedness and achieve awareness of your true essence.

This is the moment in which you reach an insight into the true nature of all things and your own self, and discover your mind-ox within yourself. You have passed through the gate to Kensho, the primal insight of the self, and have once more found your mind-ox, your true self!

In the Pi-yen-lu, the "Blue Cliff Record" from the twelfth century, one of the most important texts of Zen literature with a collection of a hundred koans, there is the following saying by the Chinese Zen Master Yuan-wu:

> Completely clear and obvious – the ox in the open field. Keen eyes and open ears it has. But tell me: what is the ox in the open field?

> **There stands the ox, no longer can anything conceal it. Yet which artist can paint this majestic head with its magnificent horns?**

This passage in our poem from the third ox-herding picture does indeed sound like a poetic addendum, yet in truth it provides a clue of great significance. The poem describes the ox's majestic head with its magnificent horns, although only the hindquarters can be seen in the picture. Its head is hidden between the tall grasses and shrubs. This signifies that in this fleeting moment of primal insight, your mind has not yet achieved consummate clarity. On this level, you can only perceive a minimal partial aspect of reality because your mind is still caught in the tangle of discriminating thinking. However, if you want to perceive and paint the whole mind-ox, with its majestic head and magnificent horns, you yourself must become the mind-ox – you must realise your true self. To this, a story from ancient China:

A painter who was honoured in the kingdom of China as a great artist was given a commission by the emperor to paint a great painting of a dragon for him which should appear very alive. Yet despite all efforts, the painter was not able to produce such a painting with a lively-looking dragon. Many months passed and the emperor became more and more impatient.

One day, while the painter was standing, filled with despair in front of yet another unsuccessful painting, a huge dragon suddenly stretched its head through the window and spoke to the terrified painter, "You can struggle all you like but if you want to paint me as I really am, you must completely forget yourself and become the dragon yourself."

The following occurrence with Zen Master Nansen clearly illustrates this too:

> When Zen Master Nansen lay dying, his highest monk asked him, "What will have become of you in a hundred years?" Nansen,

"A water buffalo at the foot of this mountain."
The monk, "May I follow you there?" Nansen,
"If you wish to do that, you must hold a tuft
of grass in your muzzle!"

If you wish to follow old Master Nansen too, whether you like it or not, there is only one possibility for you: "When your apparent personality – the ego delusion - dies, you must become the water buffalo, the mind-ox yourself." In the words of the Christian mystic Meister Eckhart, who was closely akin to Zen, "If a person wishes to experience God, he must forget himself and all things."

Yet, as long as you derive your identity from your intellect, your whole life is determined exclusively by the personality-delusion, the ego. Thus, when, through a lack of spiritual clarity, you identify yourself with your intellect and its discriminating, conceptual thinking, you are a prisoner of the space-time illusion and are stuck in the straightjacket of your self-induced concepts.

This misinterpretation leads to a tremendous number of negative ramifications since it is the real cause of all human suffering. For as long as you do not recognise your true self and do not know who you really are, your thinking creates an imagined, personified personality with its tendency of grasping and rejecting. This pseudo-self, created by your ignorance as a replacement for your true self, is full of fears and needs since it is constantly doing its best to sustain its false feeling of a self.

That is the reason why you are constantly putting up resistance against everything which could endanger the stability and integrity of your false feeling of a self. This dualistic state of mind then causes all interpersonal conflicts, as well as all other conflicts, and thus suffering for yourself and others.

The root of your illusions and suffering is therefore to be found solely in your preference for yourself, brought about by the ego-delusion. Without this autonomous, habitual concept of an identifying ego-notion there is no duality and thus there is no delusion of a personality, existing of its own accord. For what you in general believe to be your own personality is in truth nothing more than a process of mental-physical phenomena, devoid of all reality. All your memories, everything which you identify with in your ignorance, beginning with the first day of your childhood, all the interwoven memories of your dead past, form your assumed individuality.

In this way, the false self, the ego-delusion, which defines itself through discriminating thinking, clings tightly to the illusion of time since it is frighteningly aware that the present moment of "now" would mean its dissolution and thus its certain death. Therefore it does everything in its power to sustain the illusion of time and is constantly trying to strive forth from the presence of now.

This dualistic thinking, caught in the illusion of time, causes your consciousness to experience itself as separate from everything it perceives and thus the misconceptions accumulate, one upon the other. I and you arise, right and wrong, good and evil, and you are trapped in the tangle of your discriminating, conceptual thinking. Consequently, your apparent personality is nothing more than a marionette, hanging from the threads of your own conditionings.

"Be here now, turn your mind around and behold your true countenance before your birth", says Zen. Everything else is just needless energy consumption and a pure waste of time. For all analysing why this is so or not so and who or what you are, only manoeuvres you all the more into the creeping snarl of the samsaric cycle of birth and death. And remember: just when you are in great confusion, death can befall you.

Therefore, see things as they really are, without the concept of your dualistic interpretation. That is the correct, non-identifying perspective of a Zen practitioner, that is the way to the all-perfecting clarity of the mind. When you have found the mind-ox, your true essence, in the primal insight of the self, "Kensho", you are aware of your primordial, true essence and you achieve of state of consciousness of crystal-clear awareness of mind.

In this experience, you are in unison with yourself and all things. Your consciousness is no longer that of separateness in the sense of "here am I and there is the world". Instead, you now understand that your mind is all things, and all things are a phenomenon of your own true self.

> This unity is like salt in water and colour in ink. Not even the smallest thing is different from the true self.

However valuable this experience, which is often wrongly held for Satori may be, we must not forget in the process that this is "not yet the true, great Enlightenment experience", as is the case with true Satori. Although a true Kensho experience, as an insight into your own essence, presents a high state of spiritual achievement, it is nevertheless as far from it as the heavens from the earth. For Satori is far more than an intuitive understanding of the true self, as in a Kensho experience, since the one who experiences Satori dissolves completely into Satori. By viewing the mind-ox in this third ox-herding picture, in a fleeting, short moment of primal insight, you have experienced Kensho, the essence of your true nature, so that your spiritual eye has opened.

All the same, you have yet to die the mystical Great Death, in which the ego-delusion is completely extinguished and you arise from the dead. For true life only begins with the death of the ego. Only then do you truly begin to live. What is more, Kensho can be experienced at different levels and one must consider that most experiences of Kensho are very shallow and to a certain extent still take place on an intellectual level. Some of those who think they have seen the ox, have in truth only seen the end of the ox's tail. But most of them, filled with pride, claiming they have experienced Kensho, have in fact only seen a goat and then try to ride home on this goat. This shows that on this level, one is not yet truly armed against falsities. Even when you have "Glimpsed", as Zen puts it, and have had a mystical experience, perhaps Kensho – continue on! The Chinese Zen Master Han-shan (seventeenth century) says of this:

> Many of those who practise Zen often only attain a superficial realisation without depth. Worst of all is when they settle for such a small, superficial realisation without depth.

The old Chinese Zen masters never made such a great fuss over a small Kensho experience as it is common today in Japanese Zen monasteries. These days, even when a Zen student has only experienced an insignificant glimpse, a certificate of Enlightenment, Inka-Shomei is conferred on him forthwith. Yet to make this very clear: the light of the One Mind shines forth only when everything that is blocking the light, however small it is, has been swept out of the way. Even the smallest obstacle and the tiniest misconception must be swept away because the biggest is equal to the smallest and the smallest is equal to the biggest.

> A monk asked Master Chih-chang, "Who is Buddha?"
> The master replied, "Would you believe me if I told you?"
> The monk, "Why should I not?"
> The master, "You are him."
> The monk, "How can I recognise this?"
> The master, "When just a single grain of dust is in your eye, all sorts of deceptive phenomena will plague you."

What you are seeking is your true, divine self, beyond space and time and beyond birth and death. It is your own reality. You have never lost it, it is always there. You have only covered it with the projections of your discriminating, conceptual thinking. That is why Zen Master Huang-po gives you the following good piece of advice: "The mind is filled with radiant clarity so cast away the darkness of your old, dead concepts. Free yourself of everything!"

IV.

Harnessing the Ox

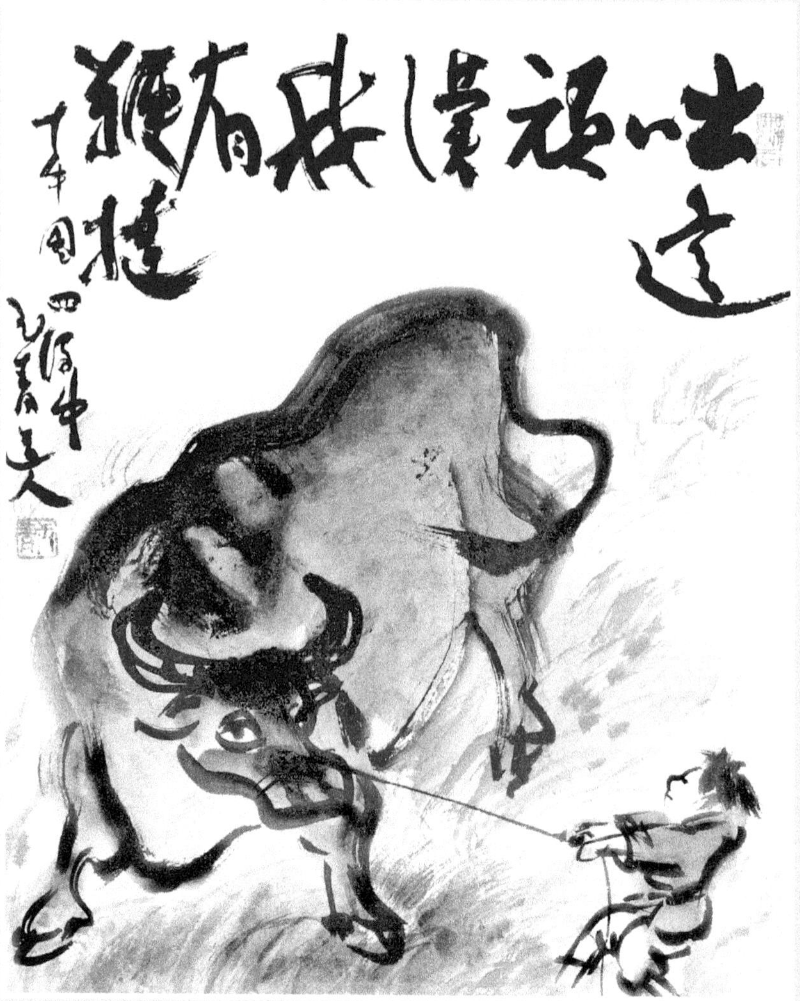

Poem and annotation by Kakuan

Firmly he grips the ox's reins and holds on tight with all his strength. Its will is still too strong and its power still too tumultuous for him to banish its wildness.
It storms aloft to the higher plains, high above the misty clouds or it stands in a pathless gorge.

Today he has captured the ox, which had been hiding in the wilderness for a long time. With great effort he has harnessed it, yet the ox does not follow him, for it is enamoured by the familiar, pleasant wilderness, to which it is still strongly drawn. Filled with desire for the sweetly fragrant grass, it wanders off. Its spirit is still too wild and headstrong. If he wants to subjugate it, he must draw his whip.

Comment by Zensho

Firmly he grips the ox's reins and holds on tight with all his strength. Its will is still too strong and its power still too tumultuous for him to banish its wildness.

Kakuan adds to this his commentary:

Today he has captured the ox, which had been hiding in the wilderness for a long time. With a great effort he has harnessed it, yet the ox does not follow him.

In Zen practice it is not enough that, having experienced primal insight, Kensho, your true essence, you catch sight of the mind-ox and then sit back in comfort and now believe that this is everything. Even though you have beheld your mind for a brief moment, you must not stop here.

Instead, you must now capture and tame your refound ox if you wish to ride home on it. Of course, this is easier said than done. For in this consciousness state you do not yet have any real power over the mind-ox and without intensive Zen practice, the ox quickly runs off again and evades your perception.

It storms aloft to the higher plains, high above the misty clouds or it stands in a pathless gorge.

In his commentary on this fourth ox-herding picture, Kakuan says:

For it is enamoured by the familiar, pleasant wilderness, to which it is still strongly drawn. Filled with desire for the sweetly fragrant grass, it wanders off. Its spirit is still too wild and headstrong. If he wants to subjugate it, he must draw his whip.

Subjugating the ox means that you must now make sure that the mind does not fall back once more into its familiar concept of its old way of seeing and doing things. You have indeed caught the ox but the mind-ox is still not in harmony with you.

When it sees and smells the sweet fragrant grass, it runs to the green meadow and does not want to come back. As long as it is still so wild and uncontrolled you are far from being in harmony with it and you cannot ride home on it. Although, for a moment your true essence revealed itself to you in Kensho, it is not yet possible for you to master the ox, your mind, such as you wish. For you are not yet free from your intellectual discrimination, your passions and the egocentric cravings. You are still caught in the old concepts of your subjective notions and your emotionally tainted thinking. Your ox is still too wild and tumultuous and wants to drag you back by the harness into the familiar world of opposites.

Yet only when you tame your mind-ox and really become free from the compulsions of discriminating, conceptual thinking, and thoughts no longer attach to anything, whatever it is, will you achieve a true understanding of Zen. The truth of Zen can only unfold in a mind which is completely free from all concepts and the compulsion of autonomous, discriminating thinking. For all discrimination between this and that turns you into a slave of your self-created mental projections and consequently, you will only distance yourself all the more from the truth.

Indeed, only when the mind has been cleansed of the tangle of discriminating, conceptual thinking will the radiating blaze of the unblemished One Mind reveal itself in the experience of Enlightenment. In contrast to Satori, the great Enlightenment experience in which the ego-delusion is completely eradicated in the Great Death, in the Kensho experience the ego continues to exist.

For this reason, there is constantly the great danger with a Kensho experience that the insight you have now gained will suffocate in the tangle of habitual, discriminating thinking and will become increasingly forgotten. Worst of all is that at some point, no more remains than the empty memory of an experience you once had.

Thus, there is the inescapable necessity following a Kensho experience – and naturally before one as well – of stabilising your spiritual self-awareness through the practice of Zen meditation, Zazen, in order to achieve constant awareness of mind, everywhere and at all times.

In Zen, this practice is known as "capturing and taming the ox". After you have found the mind-ox within you, you must now be aware of it everywhere and at all times, and be completely one with it.

In intentionless self-awareness of the mind, this oneness must become your absolute, natural state of mind. However, this is only possible when you do not cling to the "false Zen practice" of silently sitting still, in which you suppress all thoughts. The old Chinese Zen masters called this "the dead Zen of the spirit cave of the dead void".

Many who practise Zen allow themselves to be deceived and seriously take this "pitfall of the dead void" to mean they have achieved a higher state of immersion. As a result, they often linger in this state for long periods of time without realising that their spiritual awareness is becoming increasingly dull and sluggish instead of gaining in sharpness and clarity. The Chinese Zen Master Po-chan (seventeenth century) therefore warns us:

> During Zen meditation, many people are constantly striving to arrest their thoughts and they forcibly suppress their minds. As soon as distracting thoughts surface, they are promptly chased away. Even the weakest thought impulses are immediately suppressed. This false kind of practice and understanding represents the biggest trap into which Zen adherents can fall: "The pitfall of the dead void". Such people are the living dead. They become dull, indifferent, unfeeling and lethargic.

If you truly wish to achieve liberation, you must progress at all costs beyond this false practice of calming the mind. At best, its practice will lead to your thoughts being temporarily switched off or to a state of yoga-sleep. Here, there is no real perception, no understanding and no vivacious experiencing of your original, true essence.

Therefore, during meditation, do not make the mistake of wanting to suppress the thoughts. For when you try to suppress thoughts, the mind just reacts with increased mental activity. So remain totally relaxed and view each arising thought directly, without attaching to it. Do not be concerned when distracting thoughts arise, but remain sharply aware so that you do not recognise them when it is too late. This way, with the "sword of perfect awareness of mind", you will be able to slice through each arising flow of thoughts in a flash.

An essential word in Zen is "intentionlessness". Thus, when you are meditating, be completely intentionless, for as soon as you have the intention to not think, a state of psychological-physical tension always arises because tension is suppressed desire. It is fundamentally important that you do not manipulate the mind but rather leave it as it is. Leave the mind in its original true nature. All attempts to correct it by means of intervention are wrong and only lead to mental exhaustion. That is why Zen says, "Be like an old incense burner in an old abandoned village temple."

Abide during Zen meditation, Zazen, in intentionless, crystal-clear awareness of mind and let your breathing flow freely. This is how you reach your centre and abide, concentrated within yourself.

Zen breathing is deep, easeful breathing, in which the focus lies in the lower abdomen. In this region, known in Zen as "Hara", we experience a feeling of stability and accumulated energy during Zazen, which is very helpful for maintaining spiritual awareness.

Correct breathing in Zen meditation is very important, for the mind becomes clear like the cloudless sky through deep, tranquil breathing in and out. Breathe during Zazen as naturally as possible, but pay attention that you are aware when breathing out and that your breathing out is considerably longer than your breathing in.

Generally speaking, people are not aware of their breathing and thus their breathing in and out takes place quite automatically. Yet in the practice of Zen meditation it is an unavoidable requirement for you to breathe consciously. Therefore, breathe in and out consciously and observe whilst you do so the tranquil, smooth flowing of the breathing. This conscious, attentive breathing is the bullwhip of awareness which holds the mind-ox in the absolute presence of now, so that the mind strengthens and your thinking can no longer take on a life of its own.

This ongoing practice of aware breathing leads you to a "Samadhi of breathing", in which the breathing transcends itself so that it is no longer consciously perceived. However, as long as you are still aware of your breathing, you are yet to have a truly deep Samadhi, for in this state of consciousness it would not be possible for you to perceive your breathing. Ultimately, it is about achieving crystal-clear awareness, in which you are so One with the breathing that you are no longer aware of your breathing.

When thoughts arise, be aware of their empty nature. Let the thoughts and inner images pass by like clouds in the sky, without any regard to them or trying to grasp them. Be completely indifferent to what takes place in the mind, yet "remain in so doing in crystal-clear awareness" and turn your consciousness to focus on your essence behind the thinking.

Thus, when you do not supply any more nourishment to the thoughts by no longer taking any notice of them, they will dissolve like snowflakes in warm water. This is how you achieve clarity of mind in your ongoing practice of Zen meditation, so that through your own experience, you increasingly understand that all phenomena arise in your own mind.

By understanding the insubstantiality of all phenomena you perceive that they are empty, and so it is no longer possible for you to maintain the habitual notion of an external world of phenomena.

The result of this is that your identification with this attachment to things decreases. By recognising the deceptive nature of all phenomena you become free from your concepts and see things clearly as they are.

During meditation, do not think of before and after. Completely extinguish your memory of the past, forget the future, forget your body and your mind. In this instant of direct present there is neither space nor time – only absolute, eternal Now exists.

Retain this pure state of continuous, highly alert awareness by abiding in the direct presence of Now. Let the present instant be your only true life. Through this you achieve a constant, uninterrupted, intentionless self-awareness of mind. It is the experience of direct, naked perception of the crystal-clear nature of the mind in each moment of your daily life. Thus, when you are constantly aware of your own, original mind, each of your actions takes place entirely spontaneously and naturally. This way, your true, original buddha-nature will develop in the course of your spiritual realisation.

Therefore, it is fundamentally important for your spiritual practice on the Zen path that you do not just practise the sitting meditation of Zen now and again but that you return to it regularly. "Joriki", the power of your spiritual concentration develops from your meditation, together with the ability to constantly retain your spiritual awareness. This uninterrupted self-awareness of mind was referred to by the old Chinese Zen masters as "the herding of the cow".

> When the future Zen Master Shih-kung (eighth century) was still a student of his master Ma-tsu, he was working one day in the kitchen when the master entered and asked him what he was doing there.
> "I am herding the cow", said the student.
> "How do you guard it?" asked the master.
> "When it deviates for a moment from the path, I lead it by the nose straight back and leave it no time to linger!"
> The master replied, "You truly know how to herd the cow."

Through this holistic "Zen practice of cow-herding" you gain the ability to spontaneously adapt to all situations and to act accordingly, without losing the tranquillity of your spiritual awareness in the process. For tranquillity and motion are not mutually exclusive. On the contrary, they complement each other, and in the midst of our modern world, they must be experienced as an inseparable unit. Only so can the spiritual rhythm appear which pervades heaven and earth. You must go the path to liberation in the midst of the world. For how can you learn to swim apart from in water? How can you overcome the world apart from in the world? The Zen way only has a meaning when you place a foot on it and truly follow it.

That is active, vivacious Zen. That is the true Zen way. Experiencing our original, true essence, the original state of the mind in the midst of the world is the way of the "fire lotus". In Zen, the powerful image of the fire lotus is readily used here as opposed to the water lotus, which only grows in an untouched, silent pond. As an example of this, the Chinese Zen Master Yung-chia (eighth century) says:

> The power of true wisdom proves itself precisely in practising the Zen way amidst the fire of the world. This lotus flower, which blossoms from out of the fire, is eternally unwithering.

Therefore, always bear in mind that active participation in the world and silent awareness of mind do not obstruct one another and are not irreconcilable opposites. You only make two out of them when you distinguish between worldly and spiritual life. In the words of Zen Master Lin-chi: "While you love what is holy and loathe what is common, you are still bobbing up and down in the sea of ignorance."

Essential on the vivacious, active Zen way of the fire lotus is that you reach such a state of consciousness of equanimity and an unshakable mind that you are able to retain the spiritual stability you have gained in Zen meditation even in particularly distracting external circumstances. In so doing, you achieve a continuation of Zen practice in all the activities of daily life, in which it is no longer a case of what you do but rather of your consciousness, that is to say, your "awareness" during the activity. And thus you abide in each of life's situations in a detached, relaxed attitude of steadfastness of mind.

Achieving equanimity is one of the essential elements in the spiritual practice of Buddhism. In Zen, equanimity means "perfect mastery of the mind-ox". This means that in the midst of the hustle and bustle of daily life you are able to adapt yourself to all changes, act as the situation requires, and at the same time remain completely at ease. Thus, in all situations of daily life, even when they arise suddenly and unexpectedly, you will be capable of making clear decisions and acting on these decisions in a correct way.

In Mahayana-Buddhism, equanimity also has another, profounder meaning. For the realisation of higher equanimity requires a profound, unprejudiced understanding of those beings, trapped in their ignorance. As opposed to indifference, equanimity means that from your experience of consubstantiality with all beings, you live in all-encompassing compassion in the midst of the world of Samsara and are constantly willing to help others to liberation. And anyway, all-encompassing compassion, "Karuna", is an essential precondition on the path to Enlightenment. For this reason, the key thought of Mahayana-Buddhism is "Bodhichitta", the "mind of Enlightenment".

Bodhichitta is "active wisdom" and means striving for Enlightenment for the welfare of all living beings, with the desire to liberate all beings from their subjugation to the cycle of birth and death. However, as long as you only strive for your own Enlightenment and think, "I want to achieve Enlightenment and put this world behind me, I don't want to have anything more to do with those people living mindlessly in spiritual ignorance", you will never achieve Enlightenment.

You can strive for millions of incarnations on the spiritual path but you will never experience Enlightenment this way, for breaking through to this great, liberating awakening is precluded by the profound insight into the all-embracing wholeness of being and non-separateness of all beings. This requires a fundamental spiritual attitude of opening oneself without reservation to life in its universality. Such holistic openness encompasses inner compassion for the pain and torment of all suffering beings.

This experience of consubstantiality leads to the wish to achieve Enlightenment in order to help all beings reach liberation. For you can only help others achieve liberation when you yourself are liberated. Then their eye of wisdom opens and they recognise that they have been buddhas from the very beginning on. In the language of Zen, the powerful words of the Chinese Zen Master Mumon (thirteenth century) express this so:

> A thunderclap in a clear blue sky. All earthly beings have opened their eyes. Everything beneath the sun has bowed at once.

The instant you awaken, you know that all beings have been Buddha from the beginning on, without knowing it. When you awaken from your samsaric dream of a three dimensional world in space and time, you recognise that "Everything is the One Mind, beside which nothing else exists."

V

Taming the Ox

牧去東　收起　自牧人

Poem and annotation by Kakuan

Whip and rein are required,
he must not let go for one instant or the ox would run off along the dusty road.
However, well tamed, it becomes patient and docile.
Without rope and reins it willingly follows the herder.

When a thought arises, so others follow. When the mind awakens, everything becomes clear. In mental confusion everything is untrue.
Things do not obtain their existence through the external world, for they emerge solely in the own mind. The herder must hold on tightly to the reins and must not allow any hesitant doubting to arise.

Comment by Zensho

Whip and rein are required,
he must not let go for one instant or the ox
would run off along the dusty road.

In the instant of primal insight you have refound and captured your ox. Yet now it is absolutely necessary for you to tame your unruly ox. Taming takes place in a complete transformation of the uncontrolled, wild and stubborn nature of the ox to a state of placidity and submissiveness. However, without a strong will, together with heightened awareness, you will not be able to master your mind-ox.

The term "herder's reins" denotes the strong will of your inner spiritual strength, with which you prevent your mind-ox from fleeing into the familiar realm of its old concepts. For your familiar, blinded way of viewing things and way of acting have become so fixed in your mind that it is not so easy to dissolve them.

Thus, without the "whip of awareness" it will not be possible for you to tame your mind-ox. Zen Master Yuan-wu (twelfth century) therefore gives this good advice: "From the moment onwards when you rise in the morning, exercise correct awareness and keep your mind silent; and whatever you say or do, observe it carefully and watch where it comes from and what it is that causes all your saying and doing."

> When a thought arises, so others follow. When the mind awakens, everything becomes clear.
> In mental confusion everything is untrue.

One thought and then another thought, and soon all emotions appear, bringing a multitude of problems with them. Yet when emotions arise, spiritual clarity is lost and you end up in terrible confusion. In other words: When your mind moves, all things arise, and when your mind is at rest within itself, all things disappear. Yet what is this movement of the mind?

The movement of the mind is the agitation on the surface of the mind-ocean, caused by your dualistic perspective of accepting and rejecting. As a consequence, waves of discriminating thinking arise.

This consequence is at the same time causation, for when thoughts arise, emotions arise too, and when emotions arise, further thoughts follow and your spiritual awareness becomes lost. This process of self-perpetuating thoughts and emotions continues unabated until finally, you completely lose yourself in the flow of an unrelenting stream of thoughts. Therefore, it is extremely important to develop an alert awareness through the power of your concentration, which protects you from distractions and mental lethargy. Thus, become an observer of your thoughts with their constantly repeating, conditioned thought-patterns, and your thinking will lose its obsessiveness. This way, you will free yourself from your unconscious, dualistic perspective, together with the automatic compulsion to discriminate and judge.

When you notice you are lingering on something and something bothers or inhibits you, there are always false conceptions involved. However, if you were to reach an awareness free from thinking, through the Zen practice of taming the mind-ox, so that your mind is empty and clear like empty space, you would instantly break the chain of cause and result.

Thus, free yourself from your self-perpetuating compulsion of discriminating, problem-causing, conceptual thinking and your true essence will reveal itself in its original purity. This, your birth- and deathless true essence in its original purity is the brightly radiating "Dharmakaya", the reality of the One Mind, beside which nothing else exists. This means that everything you perceive in the world, even the apparent solidity of material, is nothing more than an illusory notion of the mind. Therefore, it is written in the annotation to the fifth poem:

Things do not obtain their existence through the external world, for they emerge solely in the own mind.

Everything you perceive and experience is not real, and is instead a product of your projecting mind. Consequently, the external world of phenomena, indeed the entire cycle of birth and death is in truth, nothing other than an illusion of your own mind and not an external experience.

Yet, since the true nature of all things is just Mind and thus empty, your subjugation to the world of phenomena disappears of its own accord as soon as you see through the delusive nature of phenomena and understand the nature of your mind.

As a result, you become free by recognising that the all-embracing, pure nature of your mind and the nature of all things are perfectly One, for everything is the One Mind, beside which nothing else exists. If you wish to experience the One Mind, it is absolutely necessary that your mind becomes clear and empty, for only a clear mind can recognise itself.

Thus, if you wish to ride home on your mind-ox, you must firstly tame it and be in harmonic unison with it – "You must be completely one with it". By maintaining awareness of mind, you must ensure that the mind-ox does not deviate from the correct path.

The herder must hold on tightly to the reins and must not allow any hesitant doubting to arise.

However, well tamed, it becomes patient and docile.
Without rope and reins it willingly follows the herder.

After a long, arduous struggle with the mind-ox, it slowly becomes tame and is brought under control. Thus, by maintaining constant awareness, you make sure that the mind does not once again become self-perpetuating and a victim of its old concepts of wanting, rejecting and spiritual blindness. However, this can only take place through Zen practice when you constantly strive to keep your mind pure by liberating it of all blemishes. The old Chinese Zen masters called this "bathing the cow". Here, the cow is the mind-ox, which appears time and again in the mondos and koans of the old masters. It is closely related to the ox-herding pictures and has a very profound meaning in Zen. In Zen, bathing the cow means "a state of mind of constant, uninterrupted awareness with continual perception of the own mind". This can be clearly seen in the following example:

The Chinese Zen Master Nansen (ninth century) went along to the bathtub and asked the monk in charge of heating the water, "What are you doing there?" The monk replied, "Heating the water." Nansen said, "When you have finished, do not forget to call the cow and bath it." The monk replied, "I shall".

The same evening, this monk entered Nansen's room. Nansen asked, "What are you doing here?" The monk answered, "I am here to tell the cow that its bath is ready." Nansen asked, "Do you have its harness with you?" The monk was speechless.

When Zen Master Joshu visited Nansen, he told him about this. Joshu spoke, "I have something to say about it." Nansen asked, "Do you have the harness with you?" That instant, Joshu grabbed Nansen's nose and pulled it. Nansen said, "Alright, alright – why be so brutal?"

Old Joshu really did have the harness with him. And when he grabbed Master Nansen's nose, he made it unmistakeably clear that he was well in control of his mind-ox. Zen is always refreshingly direct and does not digress in pleasant words and friendly fussings, aimed at uplifting the ego. Zen has but one goal: it wishes to thoroughly destroy all your attachments to words, notions and expectations so that you awaken from the dream of being bound to the cycle of birth and death.

Although reality is directly before you, right there where you currently are, you pass it by and do not immerse yourself in it, and thus you are not able to experience it. This is the reason why all the various religious thought-systems with their clever elucidations have arisen. Yet these are no more than pleasant, consoling means to prevent children from whining. Everything is there – nothing is lacking, there is nothing to seek and nothing to gain. All that matters is an adjustment of consciousness. This is the only way you can overcome your habitual, everyday, "monkey-like consciousness" that becomes restless when it has nothing to cling to and jumps from one agitated thought to the other, just like a monkey jumping from one branch to the next.

In Buddhism, the monkey is a symbol for the restless consciousness. That is why, in the Buddhist iconography of the Pratitya-Samutpada, the great wheel of dependant emergence of birth, aging, despair, illness, pain, and death, you can see a monkey tied to a tree so that it can no longer move. This means that as soon as your consciousness comes to rest, the mind becomes calm. When the tendency of grasping and rejecting no longer ruffles the surface of the consciousness-ocean like the wind causing a thousand waves, the surface will become still and calm.

With the crystal clear vision of the unmoved mind, you will then be able to see down to the bottom of the mind-ocean and perceive your true face before your birth. Your task is to raise this mysterious sacred treasure but you will only be able to recognise it when you stop wallowing around in the ocean of consciousness, so that you no longer cause waves to be created which cover the fundamental, true self-mind.

So let go of everything, forget your body and your mind – forget yourself! Yet, this is not something you can do wilfully, but only when you relax into the present moment of "now".

In this absolute presence of Now you become open for the pure light of absolute consciousness. The moment this letting go occurs, the reality of your original, true essence before your birth shines forth and you recognise that this radiating light of the One Mind is not separate from you but your true, eternal self.

To reach this wonderful experience of your true, original nature is it therefore necessary for you to make your whole life a life in the direct presence of absolute "now". Ultimately, it is about liberating yourself from all your conditionings and thus all thought models and their resulting behaviour patterns. Yet, since conditionings are always the result of conceptual thinking, Zen Master Huang-po gives us the following advice:

> Just desist from the fallacy of intellectual or conceptual thought processes, and your true essence will reveal itself in its original purity. This alone is the way to Enlightenment.

VI.

Returning home on the Ox's back

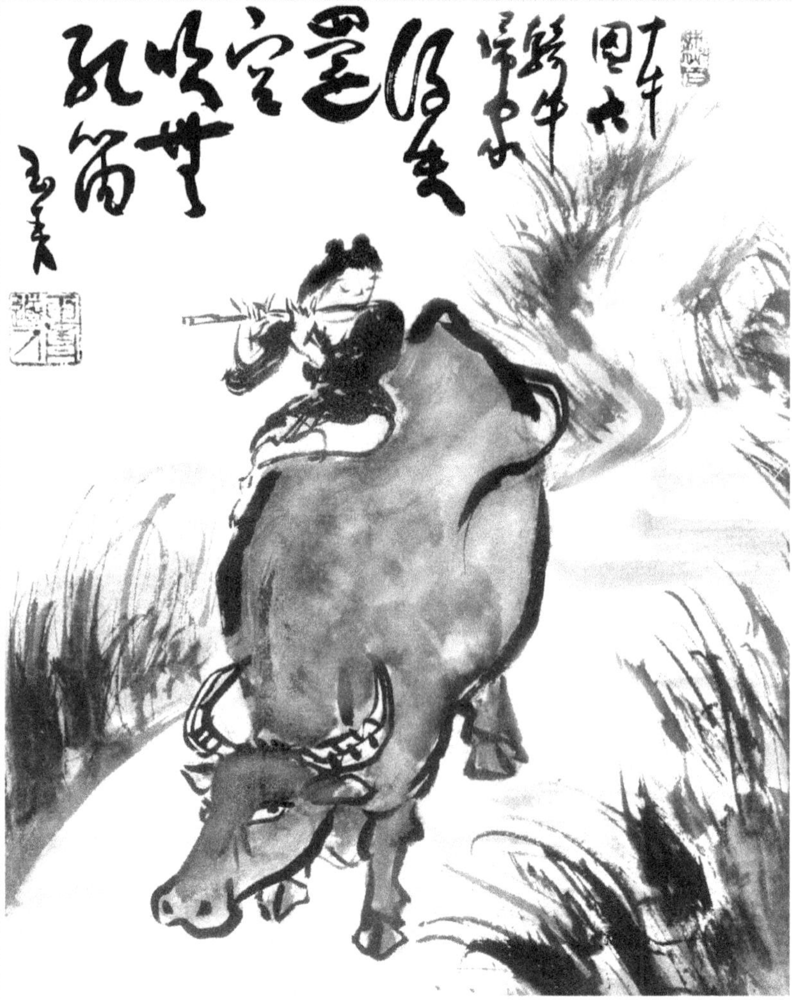

Poem and annotation by Kakuan

In cheerful serenity he rides sedately back home on the ox's back.
In the distant, receding evening mists the sound of his flute continues to resound.
The verse in time with his song,
is endlessly deep in meaning.
Does he still need words,
who understands the deep meaning?

The struggle is finally over. Gain and loss have dissolved into the void. The herder sings a rural melody and plays on the flute the simple songs of the village children. He sits on the ox's back and looks up cheerfully to the clouds in the sky.
If one calls back to him, he does not turn round. If one wishes to stop him, he does not linger.

Comment by Zensho

In cheerful serenity he rides sedately back home on the ox's back.

In this state of mind, known in Zen as "the cheerful-relaxed reflection of the mind", you have achieved an effortless, silent awareness of the mind-ox. This is a state of continuous inner peace, together with clear, effortless awareness of mind.

The Taoist sage Lao-tse says of this, "This is a returning to the root and means stillness. Stillness means: returning to destiny. Returning to destiny means: eternity." In the poetic words of the Chinese Zen Master Hung-chih (twelfth century):

> Silent and in cheerful serenity, all words are forgotten – brilliantly clear and full of life it appears before you. When you become aware of it, it is immeasurable and without beginning or end. Only in its intrinsic light do you truly become aware of everything.
>
> This radiating consciousness is an exceptional mirror, this pure reflection is full of wonders. The dew and the moon, the stars and the rivers, the snow and the pines, and the clouds which hover above the mountain tops.

Out of the gloom, they all transform into radiating brightness; out of darkness they all become gleaming light. Endless miracles await and weave in this cheerful serenity.

When you have reached a perception of your true self through effortless, crystal-clear awareness of mind, it is difficult for you to fall back into your old behaviour patterns and way of seeing things. In this mental state you are aware of the mind-ox as your own true self. By realising this crystal-clear awareness, only the present exists. You have become completely one with this present moment. The observer and the observed flow together into one. The observer becomes the observed.

Nevertheless, this is not yet highest realisation since in this experience, the mind-ox "is still there" in your conscious awareness. Although it is hardly noticeable, it is nonetheless a great hindrance on the path to Enlightenment. For on your path to complete liberation of the mind, you must put everything behind you, whatever it may be, and ultimately Buddha as well. Zen Master Pai-chang (ninth century) tells us this too: "As long as you still have a Buddha, you are still bound to birth and death." And Meister Eckhart says of this: "For this I pray to God to rid me of God."

*He sits on the ox's back and looks up cheerfully
to the clouds in the sky.
If one calls back to him, he does not turn round.
If one wishes to stop him, he does not linger.*

This is the stage where you return to harmonic unison with the all-embracing wholeness of being. Subject and object, the seer and the seen, person and mind-ox are all on the path back to the great One.

At the start of the picture series, the ox and the herder are still two. Then they grow more and more together into unity. Here, there is no turning back and you stride unwaveringly towards your destiny of great liberation from birth and death. Thus it is written in the annotation to the poem:

The struggle is finally over. Gain and loss have dissolved into the void.

The struggle with your mind-ox is over, but this is not yet "the great liberation" for you have yet to experience Satori – Enlightenment.

The fruit of your spiritual practice has appeared on the tree of spiritual realisation, but it is still too small and not yet ripe. Nonetheless, you have put a great deal of your old concepts behind you and have reached the consciousness state for returning to the origin of all being. Cheerfully relaxed, you ride leisurely back home on your mind-ox – but you have not yet arrived.

Having caught a glimpse of the mind-ox in our third picture, you were accorded an initial brief view of your true nature. In the course of your spiritual maturation process in the fourth and fifth ox-herding pictures, you little by little reached a deeper insight into your true nature. Yet, even though the Zen ox-herding pictures portray various stages of spiritual development, we must not assume we are dealing with different grades of Enlightenment.

"There is no gradual Enlightenment! It does not have different grades; it takes place all at once." This is a key statement of the true, original Zen of the old Chinese masters, such as the great giants of Zen: Huang-po, Lin-chi, Ma-tsu, Hui-neng, and many others.

The great Enlightenment experience is like the sudden blossoming of the lotus flower and is like the sudden awakening of a dreamer. Enlightenment always happens in an instant and completely unexpectedly, for it is an absolute moment-experience. If it does not take place suddenly and in an instant, it is no true Enlightenment experience.

The experience of Enlightenment cannot be achieved by extending and clinging on to self-awareness by sitting crossed-legged for hours on end, as the adherents of a one-sided sitting-dogmatism believe. Instead, it is only achieved when the attachment to this awareness has been completely eradicated. The perfect, non-substantial enlightened void will only reveal itself to you as the radiating magnificence of the One Mind when you have transcended this.

Yet to reach this wonderful experience of great Enlightenment, inevitably, you must first go through the experience which is known in Zen as "the Great Death". In the words of the Chinese Zen Master Ta-hui (twelfth century):

> Only when you let your mind drop headlong into the fathomless deep where intellect and thinking can never reach, and you die the Great Death, will you behold the absolute, radiating One Mind. This is the only way for you to achieve liberation from the cycle of birth and death.

True spiritual practice is a matter of life and death, and is ultimately about the death of the ego. You will only perceive your true essential-nature by radically turning inwards and dying into your deepest essential-ground. For you can only experience the fullness of being when you have been renewed through the baptism of mystical death.

However, without tenacity on the path to liberation and without the spiritual guidance of an enlightened master you cannot reach Enlightenment. For Zen is a direct transmission of the light, from mind to mind. In Zen tradition, this takes place in a direct, secret transmission from Heart-Mind to Heart-Mind, "Ishin-Denshin", from master to student. The Chinese Zen Master Huang-po says of this:

> There is no understanding through words,
> but only a transmission from mind to mind.
> For there is naught but a mysterious silent comprehension.

This is the reason why is it very rare for anyone to reach Enlightenment without the guidance of an enlightened master. However, to receive instruction from a Zen master, it is necessary to have the true mental attitude of the beginner's mind "Soshin". It is this open mental attitude in which it is clear to the Zen student that as long as he has not yet realised his true nature – the mind-ox – he knows nothing. This is an absolute necessity if he is to let go of all his fond notions and concepts and thus achieve an awakening of the mind.

When you are together with a truly enlightened master, you are in his enlightened energy field through the radiant power of his awakened mind. Yet, really, you are never separate from this enlightened energy, for it is the constantly present spiritual effective-force of your true self, only hidden behind the veil of your spiritual blindness in a way that you cannot perceive it without the blessed presence of the master.

However, when you are together with the master with an open, empty mind, you are also in harmony with the mystical radiant power of his enlightened energy, to the degree in which you open yourself to him.

Here, in the transformation process of your spiritual realisation, the eye of knowledge opens for the great mystery of your universal Essence. It opens the entrance to the endless inner space which reveals itself in its space-transcending endlessness and timeless eternity.

> In the distant, receding evening mists the sound of his flute continues to resound.
> The verse in time with his song,
> is endlessly deep in meaning.

In general, the classic Chinese flute is made of a bamboo

pipe with mouthpiece and lateral holes. However, the mysterious Zen flute is the mystical "iron flute without holes", and only he who knows how to play the stringless harp will be able to blow on the iron flute without holes.

The Zen poem of the Chinese Zen Master Hsueh-tou (eleventh century) conveys this as follows:

> The moon floats above the pine trees and the night veranda is cold. An ancient lamentation sounds from your bamboo flute which makes the listener weep.
> But the sound of the iron Zen flute without holes is beyond all sentiment. Play no more until the soundless sound of old Lao-tse fills your entire being.

One of the best known koans comes from the Japanese Zen Master Hakuin (eighteenth century), which Zen masters often use for their Zen instruction:

> When you clap two hands, you hear a sound.
> Yet what is the sound of one hand?

The soundless sound of Zen is the "truth beyond all words". It is the truth which lies beyond everything that sense and reason can comprehend, and it reveals our true essence. That is why the poem to the sixth ox-herding picture ends with the words:

> Does he still need words,
> who understands the deep meaning?

VII.

The Ox is forgotten

摩诘入不二法门，有法皆非实。

Poem and annotation by Kakuan

On the ox's back he rides home.
Yet behold, the ox is no longer to be seen.
Alone, the herder sits
in cheerful, relaxed silence.
The day is dawning,
and the red sun is already high in the sky.
The intense brilliance of the clear light
shines since time immemorial.
In his straw-covered house
whip and rein lie idle.

In the highest truth there is no duality. The herder has now understood that the ox is our original, innermost essence. When the hare is caught, you no longer need a trap. When the fish has been caught, you no longer need the net. It is as if you had freed shining gold from slag, or when the moon comes out from behind the clouds.

Comment by Zensho

On the ox's back he rides home.
Yet behold, the ox is no longer to be seen.

In the previous, sixth ox-herding picture, the herder achieved harmony with the ox. Yet now he is so one with it that he no longer needs to remind himself of it. Thus, the mind-ox is no longer perceivable as a conscious, objective experience since the herder has recognised that it is his innermost true essence.

In highest truth there is no duality. The herder has now understood that the ox is our original, innermost essence.

You only experience the mind-ox as separate from you until you have mastered it. Yet, in this ox-herding picture here, in which the ox has been mastered, the ox is completely forgotten. His conscious perception of it has now dissolved, and so the mind-ox disappears as "object" of perception from your consciousness. It is just the same in the relationship between the hare and the trap and between the fish and the net. Kakuan says:

When the hare is caught, you no longer need a trap. When the fish has been caught, you no longer need the net.

This parable, which is by the Taoist Master Dschuang-tse (third century B.C.), does not just relate to the mind-ox. Moreover, it also relates to all Buddhist teachings and Sutras. Indeed, even primal insight, Kensho and Zen are completely forgotten too. For the truth beyond all words will only reveal itself to you when you have liberated yourself from everything, whatever it may be and have become inwardly calm, empty and silent.

> Alone, the herder sits
> in cheerful, relaxed silence.
> In his straw-covered house
> whip and rein lie idle.

The mind-ox is now transcended and you are the master of your mind and are at home, meaning, you rest unwaveringly in your inner ground. It is not until this high consciousness state that the experience of Kensho really matures. Not until here can we really talk about true primal insight; a truly realised Kensho. Many Buddhists are tempted to believe that this is the highest state of being of Enlightenment.

Yet according to the truth of Zen, this consciousness state is still within the border area of Samsara, the cycle of birth and death. Although it points to a higher realisation, it is not yet great liberation.

"It is not yet great Satori", as it is in the case of true Enlightenment, since the one who experienced himself as One with the mind-ox in Kensho is still there. The mind-ox has indeed now gone but "the person remains" – and this is the essential problem! Yet Zen realisation truly takes place when both "the mind-ox and the person" have been completely forgotten. For all discrimination between relative and absolute have only gone when the mind-ox and the person have been completely forgotten.

Thus, when the person remains, as a product of the ego's imagination, it is "the greatest hindrance" to boundless liberation. That is why Zen Master Po-chan (seventeenth century) calls out:

> Bravely let go at the edge of the abyss. Resolutely and full of trust throw yourself into the abyss. Only after the death of the ego-delusion do we begin to live. This alone is the truth.

This letting go at the edge of the abyss means falling into your own depths. The water droplet falls into the ocean and dissolves into it, and you are in the all-encompassing wholeness of being. In this experience, the radiating light of your true, divine self reveals itself, which illuminates the entire universe with its light.

However, in order to reach this wonderful experience, your delusion of a personality must be completely and radically extinguished. For the root of all your problems and suffering is solely to be found in your mental confusion with the delusion of a personality, existing in its own right.

Consequently, it is the true, higher destination of your pseudo-personality to dissolve away. It is the death of the one who takes himself to be a person, and covers his eternal self by identifying with the interwoven memories of his dead past. Thus in an old Zen saying it is said: "You yourself must make the experience that the person who truly lives can only arise from the one who has died!"

So abandon the delusion of your personality-concepts once and for all and transfer your awareness from the illusory pseudo-person to the boundless empty expanse of the mind, and you will be in the fullness of the all-embracing wholeness of being.

By not recognising that this is your true, original nature, your spiritual awareness narrows to the illusion of a personality, existing in its own right.

Consequently, you cover your true essence of the boundless, transcendent mind with a myriad of concepts and notions. In doing so, you restrict yourself and are in a pitiful state of contracted consciousness. As a result, you can only perceive a tiny part, a small aspect of the whole of reality. Thus, the boundless expanse of the One Mind is narrowed to a small circle of individual ego-consciousness.

It is as if you would look at the boundless expanse of the heavens through a straw and would then take this very limited field of perception to be the entire heavens itself. Yet when the straw of your limited consciousness perspective of a self-existing personality drops, you are in the boundless expanse of the mind. Then for the first time you truly understand the profound meaning of Huang-po's words: "The One Mind and the own mind are not different, but are one sole being."

In their essence, the One Mind and the own mind are one and the same reality. Thus, perceiving the nature of the own mind means perceiving the true nature of all-embracing wholeness of being. When you perceive the mind, the mind is Buddha. When you do not perceive it, it is the ego-delusion. This perception of the One Mind is only bestowed upon you when you have freed yourself from everything, regardless of how small or beautiful or sacred it may be. Zen Master Lin-chi from the ninth century thus speaks the following powerful words:

> Clear all obstacles from the path. If you encounter Buddha, then kill Buddha! Only thus will you attain release, only thus will you escape the chains and become free.

By fulfilling a mirror-like awareness of mind with constant clarity, the dark clouds of discriminating thinking can no longer obscure your mind. This is wonderfully expressed in Kakuan's annotation to this seventh ox-herding picture:

It is as if you had freed shining gold from slag, or when the moon comes out from behind the clouds.

In the higher state of realisation of a true Kensho experience, as in this seventh ox-herding picture, the mind-ox is indeed forgotten as a conscious experience. Yet, in truth the mind-ox is still there, as it is the reality of our true being. It is the radiating splendour of the One Mind, "your original true self", beside which nothing else exists. As the original state of our mind, it is the reality which is constantly present behind all experiences.

Everything which appears as form before your eyes is the diversity of the mind's reflection. It is the One Mind, beside which nothing else exists and which remains completely untouched by all forms of change and death. Yet the "own mind", when it is bound to the concept of the delusion of a self-existing personality, is the fundamental problem of all your problems.

Accordingly, it is a great spiritual blockage when, following his Kensho experience, a person has indeed left behind the conscious awareness of his constantly present mind-ox but still clings to the self-perpetuating concept of his personality. In the language of Zen it is said: He is caught on the "gateless barrier to liberation". However, the gateless barrier has no gate, so how do you wish to go through it?

If you really want to put an end to this whole spectre, there is no other way than to awaken from the dream of body, mind and world, and thus die out of the spectacle of your projecting consciousness. That is the true way of Zen.

The moment you forget yourself and all things and immerse yourself completely in the mystical Great Death, the Great Life will be bestowed upon you. Then you will experience for the first time that something lives within you which lasts beyond birth and death and can neither drown in water or burn in fire. The following example is from the Cong-rong lu koan collection from the thirteenth century:

> A man stands on a pole, a hundred feet high – although he has achieved it, it is not yet the true goal. Up high on this hundred-foot pole you must take a step forwards!
> Then the whole universe of the ten directions is your boundless body.

The man is already at the top of the pole so how can he even go a tiny step forward? Moreover, since our entire world-experience of body, mind and world is nothing more than a dream, where should he move on to? In truth, there is no imprisonment in the cycle of birth and death and consequently, there is also no liberation to achieve. This is a very essential and fundamental thought in Zen.

For everything is the One Mind, beside which nothing else exists. Everything is MU! It really is. MU – nothing! You must become this nothing – completely be it. But do not cling to the word MU, or else you will be fixated once again. And then your MU is nothing more than a worthless thought construction without life and not the true MU of Zen.

MU is one of the central, essential concepts in Zen and represents being free from all identifications and attachments. It is the realisation of the void "Shunyata". In the well-known koan collection of the Mumonkan, "the gateless barrier" from the thirteenth century, we encounter MU in the first example with the koan of "Joshu's dog".

> A monk asks Zen Master Joshu, "Does a dog have buddha-nature?" Joshu replies, "MU!"

Joshu's MU is neither yes nor no. It is an alogical answer which surpasses the opposites yes and no, and directly points to a person's inherent buddha-nature, "absolute reality beyond all designation and discrimination". In the powerful words of Zen Master Mumon on the koan "Joshu's dog":

> Dog! Buddha-nature!
> The truth is manifested in full.
> A moment of yes and no:
> Lost are your body and soul.

The most striking feature of all koans is their alogical nature and the absurdity of the words. When people read the answers of the Zen masters to their students' questions, spoken with Zen Mind, they become confused and ask themselves what the answer has to do with the question.

However, we should make it clear to ourselves that these statements of the great Zen masters have nothing to do with any conceptual or intellectual assertation within the familiar bounds of our logical thinking. Instead we are dealing with the manifestation of a tremendous experience of such all-encompassing universality that within it, all barriers of space and time and all limitations of verbal communication are transcended.

The koan overwhelms your intellect. It causes a short circuit in your thinking and paralyses your capacity for critical discernment. For the intent and purpose of a koan is that it brings you into a spiritual borderline situation in which your intellect is trapped and you can neither move forwards nor backwards. You find yourself facing the abyss of the absolute void and your only salvation is to let go of yourself and everything, whatever it may be.

Thus, if you believe you can solve the koan MU with your intellect, you will only end up going round in circles. Those people who cling to words and sayings, interpreting MU with their intellect, and thus trying to understand it can be compared to a fool who tries to strike the moon with a stick.

Yet what is this mysterious, true MU of Zen? In his commentary on the koan "MU", Zen Master Mumon speaks these auspicious words:

> Now tell me: what is the barrier raised by the ancient masters?
>
> It is none other than this "MU". This is the Zen barrier, consequently known as the "gateless barrier" of Zen.
>
> Whoever overcomes this barrier will not only clearly see Joshu face-to-face, but can also walk hand in hand with all the masters of afore.
>
> Eyebrows touching, he sees with the same eye with which they see, and hears with the same ear with which they hear. Would it not be marvellous? Who doesn't wish to pass this marvellous barrier?

In this example from the Mumonkan, the ego-consciousness, clinging to the notion of a personality, is compared to a cow in a window:

> A cow goes through a window. Its head, its horns, its belly and its four legs are already through. How can it then be that the tail does not go through?

Zen Master Mumon appends the following verse to this wonderful koan:

> Passing through, it falls into a deep trench.
> Turning back, it is lost. This tiny little tail! –
> What a very strange and curious thing it is!

In this koan, viewed in Zen as one of the eight most difficult koans, MU appears in the form of a cow. The ancient Chinese Zen masters said: "The key to this koan is that one can only achieve great liberation through absolute obliteration of the little ego, which is still clinging on in the Kensho experience."

Yet what indeed is this extremely strange and mysterious cow tail? It is nothing other than your ego-notion, as your deepest, fundamental problem which you must solve yourself if you wish to bring the cow through the window.

By realising primal insight, Kensho, in this seventh ox-herding picture, you have indeed transcended your mind-ox as "object" of your conscious perception and thus forgotten it. But the cow, that is, your mind, is still stuck in the window of your personality concept.

Indeed, you have experienced a tremendous process of spiritual transformation, yet you are still clinging to the illusion of a self. Kensho has reached fruition but in your delusion of a self-existing personality, you are still clinging fearfully to life. Thus, your "delusion of a self", the ego, is clinging tightly. For this reason, in Buddhism, the delusion of a self is also known as Ahamkara, "the grasper and ego-maker".

However, since there is no self-existing "individual-self", the death of the ego can only mean the death of all identifications and attachments causing the ego-delusion. The fear of letting go is therefore nothing more than a result of your identification with the contents of your consciousness. By identifying with the interwoven memories of your dead past, your body and your intellect, you are convinced that this is your true essence, that is to say, your personality.

In truth, however, there is nothing more than a chain of moments of existence and combinations thereof in the form of flashes of consciousness, each one following the other in quick succession. Thus, what you generally deem to be your "I" has no reality of its own. It is merely a momentary, fleeting combination of constantly changing energies.

Our so-called individual existence, our personality, is in truth nothing more than an uninterrupted, successive process of co-acting impersonal elements of existence, with the illusion of a constant consciousness.

Yet the moment when suddenly, the contents of your consciousness disappear, and for an instant you approach the border zone of the void of the Mind, a growing feeling of identity loss will arise. Then immediately, you search panic-stricken for something you can cling to. The more you try to let go here, the more you will cling on tightly, for tension is suppressed wanting.

True letting go always happens unexpectedly and suddenly in a moment when you are completely free from intentions and do not expect it. It happens when your reach such relinquishment that this relinquishment is not something that you "do" but something that you "are". You forget yourself and all things to the point where you yourself become this "state of relinquishment". However, this takes place without wilful action on your part and happens instead by grace, "Tariki", the effective force of the One Mind.

However, as long as you still fearfully cling to life and think, "I want to immerse myself in deathlessness and die into the divine abyss, but hopefully I will come back to life", you are not yet ready for the "Great Death" – for Enlightenment. You can only experience the radiating splendour of divine being when, in complete trust, you radically die into it, without remainder. It is just the same with the water droplet, hanging from the cloud, which can only experience what the ocean is when it lets go, falls into the ocean and dissolves into it. Thus, you must reach such a state of total relinquishment that body, mind and world are truly completely forgotten. In the words of the Japanese Zen Master Dogen Zenji from the thirteenth century:

> Really understanding the true self means completely forgetting yourself; completely forgetting yourself means Enlightenment.

The barrier to absolute relinquishment is the great fear of the great void, which is a result of your self-perpetuating concept of identification with the ego-delusion. However, this fear is nothing more than an empty feeling, but when feelings arise, spiritual clarity is lost. Zen Master Huang-po says this too:

> People are afraid to relinquish their consciousness, fearing to fall through the Void with nothing to stay their fall. They do not know that the Void is not really void, but the realm of the radiating Dharmakaya. This spiritually enlightening true nature is without beginning, as ancient as the Void, subject neither to birth nor to destruction. It is all-pervading, untainted beauty. It is absolute reality, uncreated and existing of itself.

There is no other way here than to venture the leap into boundlessness and so to experience this reality. MU – nothing! You must become this nothing – completely be it. In this consciousness state of the dark night of the senses and the mind, known in Zen as "Dai-Gidan, the Great Doubt", the mind is stuck and can neither move forwards nor backwards.

The Great Doubt is an inescapable state of mind which always precedes a true Enlightenment experience. It is a form of mental barrier in which the current of thoughts falters and is unable to continue flowing. The endless abyss of the divine void opens before you and you stand on the threshold of mystical death.

This is why Zen Master Mumon says in his commentary on the koan of the cow in the window, "Passing through, it falls into a deep trench; Turning back, it is lost." In other words, when you go forwards, you fall into the unending abyss of divine nothingness. If you go back, you descend into "Samsara", the cycle of birth and death.

This is the case of a fully-matured Kensho, in which the ego is still hanging on, but by no more than a thin thread, just like ripe fruit on a tree. You are in a mental state beyond being and non-being. Zen Master Hakuin (eighteenth century) describes this situation very imposingly:

If you wish to experience your true self, you must let go when hanging from a sheer precipice. When afterwards you return to life, you experience yourself as the radiating "self-mind".

What is "to let go when hanging from a sheer precipice?" It is like a lost man who suddenly finds himself at the edge of a bottomless chasm. His feet rest precariously on a patch of slippery moss, and there is no spot on which he can steady himself. He can neither advance nor retreat; he faces only death.

The only thing he has to depend on is a thin vine that he grasps with one hand. His life is hanging by a thread. If he were suddenly to let go, not even his dried bones would be left. This is exactly how it is for the Zen practitioner. He arrives at a state in which his mind is as though dead, his volition as though extinguished; vast emptiness above a sheer precipice, no support for hands and feet. All thoughts dwindle, great fear arises in his chest.

In this situation of great doubt at the abyss of the divine Void, Zen calls out to you:

Hanging at the edge of the abyss, let go and utterly die. This is the only way to liberation.

However bleak this state may seem, it contains within it the great promise of great liberation. In the words of Zen Master Kakuan to this seventh ox-herding picture:

The day is dawning,
and the red sun is already high in the sky.
The intense brilliance of the clear light
shines since time immortal.

VIII.

Ox and Herder are forgotten

如来清浄禅
羅受不染文
十牛図
人牛俱忘

Poem and annotation by Kakuan

Whip, rein, ox and the herder
have completely dissolved into nothing.
Endlessly vast is the deep blue sky,
no words could ever describe it.
So, can a snowflake
exist in a blazing fire?
When he has reached there,
he encounters the mind of the old patriarchs
of Zen.

He is free from spiritual blindness, and all ideas of Enlightenment have vanished too. He does not abide anywhere where Buddha is to be found and where Buddha is not, he quickly passes.
Since he stops at neither of the two, even a thousand eyes cannot penetrate into his innermost essence. Even if a hundred birds would strew his path with wonderful flowers, this reverence would be completely meaningless to him.

Comment by Zensho

> Whip, rein, ox and the herder
> have completely dissolved into nothing.
> Endlessly vast is the deep blue sky,
> no words could ever describe it.

Suddenly, the power of the thinking mind is broken. From out of the depths of darkness the fullness of the light surfaces, and your true self shines in radiating clarity. This is the experience of Great Satori. The Great Death and the dissolution into the boundless expanse of being at the point of Enlightenment are one, sole experience and take place at the same time. Your original, true essence, which was hidden from you behind the clouds of your spiritual blindness, reveals itself to you in this great liberation.

Here, the mind-ox manifests itself to you in its transcendental reality with its majestic head and magnificent horns. You have returned to the origin and you recognise your original countenance before your birth, radiating as the all-illuminating buddha-nature. The Japanese Zen Master Imakita Kôsen (eighteenth century) gives us the following impressive description of his Enlightenment experience:

> One night, it was suddenly as though the

boundary between earlier and later had been cut. I entered into the marvellous realm of wondrousness. I was at the heart of the "Great Death", no perception of the existence of all things or of myself remained. All that I felt was how my body dissolved and my mind grew into boundlessness and an endless blaze of light arose.

At the moment of Enlightenment, the entire spectacle of the personal, constrained ego ceases and the fundamental unity of the one, absolute, timeless reality reveals itself to you. In experiencing this blazing clarity, you recognise that your own mind and the boundless expanse of the One Mind are a single being, beside which nothing else exists.

At one fell swoop, your true eye of Enlightenment opens, and you feel like one who has risen from the dead. Everything is realised within you and you experience yourself as the original, radiating, pure light of the One Mind, in which space and time no longer exist. In this awareness of wonderful clarity, your mind is vast and boundless. Completely whole, radiating with light, it shines brighter than a thousand suns and pervades the entire universe.

When We-dse (seventh century) called on Zen Master Hui-chung for the first time, sudden

Enlightenment was bestowed upon him in a flash. Filled with joy, he called out:

> Heaven and earth do not exist by any means, just as things and myself do not exist in any way. And yet, one cannot say that they are not real. Since this is so, both the great, enlightened wise ones as well as the common people, caught in their ignorance, are nothing more than a dream, an unreal shadow-creation. So how can there be life and death?
>
> Buddha was the one who could see this with the eye of wisdom, and thus he became the master of all things.
>
> Now that I myself am awakened, I see it myself and know that it is true.

In the instant of Great Satori, the pseudo-personality or ego-delusion still remaining after the Kensho experience now dies the Great Death and vanishes. You yourself as a person and the mind-ox as the object of your inner dedication "have completely dissolved into nothing". Everything – body, mind and world – has dissolved into the radiating void of the One Mind, beside which nothing else exists. It is the experience of absolute nothingness, in which only the pure, crystal-clear self-awareness without perceiver and without conscious perception remains.

This crystal-clear, enlightened self-awareness of mind in the experience of absolute nothingness is no longer the working of your perception but rather "pure perception itself" in its original, absolute, non-being beyond being. That is why we see the empty circle "Enso" in the eighth ox-herding picture, which in Zen represents Enlightenment, "Satori".

By awakening to the reality of your unborn, deathless, true self, the One Mind shines forth in its full brilliance as your true countenance before your birth and you are filled with great clarity and indescribable peace.

Experiencing Enlightenment is like the shattering of a rock in which one was entrapped. In a flash, everything is transformed. It is a tremendous spiritual explosion which shakes the world to its very foundations, and everything dissolves away. The entire contents of the consciousness disappear, whatever they may be. Everything – body, mind and world – vanishes. Only your true self remains and lights up the entire universe with its radiating light. For:

> So can a snowflake exist in a blazing fire?

By breaking through the gateless barrier in the instant of Great Death, all the interwoven memories of your dead past scorch to nothing in a flash, together with all concepts. The awareness of body, mind and world and the concept of the ego-notion are completely eradicated, and you are raised above all the boundaries of an earthly-bound existence in space and time. You ascend above the dark haze of the phenomena of an external world into the clear light of reality.

Everything falls away from you and you feel as though a hundredweight had been removed from your shoulders. It is the great awakening from the dream of an external world of phenomena in space and time. In this enlightened consciousness of wonderful clarity, you experience the world as though you would see it for the first time.

He is free from spiritual blindness, and all ideas of Enlightenment have vanished too.

Having realised Great Satori, the enlightened one is freed from every duality so that not even the slightest notion of Enlightenment or sacredness remains. In the Pi-yen-lu, the Blue Cliff Record, we find the following example:

The Chinese Emperor Wu-Di from Liang asked Bodhidharma, the first patriarch of Zen, "What is the profound meaning of the sacred truth?" Bodhidharma answered, "Vast emptiness, nothing sacred."

The emperor's question shows that he is still attached to the notion of sacredness. He asks this question because he believes the first patriarch of Zen standing before him to be a saintly man who is to be highly revered and who should know best of all. Yet Bodhidharma's famous answer is a tremendous blow with the sword, "Vast emptiness, nothing sacred."

In Zen there is no separation between sacred and profane. Zen does not distinguish between a spiritual life and an active life. The whole world, the whole universe is sacred, there is nothing which could not be sacred – and thus it means that nothing is particularly sacred. In other words: Vast emptiness, nothing sacred.

In the Enlightenment experience, every duality is transcended so that the enlightened one lives in perfect harmony with Tao and experiences himself as completely one with everything. He no longer experiences his true self and the self of all beings as different and separate but rather as a single being.

Thus, now he can only say, "I am you and you are me, in our true self we embrace the entire universe."

In cheerful-relaxed reflection of the mind, he lives as the one who has awakened from the dream of birth and death, beyond all discrimination, in the all-embracing wholeness of being. He abides neither in the realm of sacredness nor in the realm of misconception. For him, there is no distinction between Buddha and common people. For, in the words of Zen Master Huang-po, "Buddha and all living beings are nothing other than the One Mind, beside which nothing else exists." This is why Kakuan says:

> *He does not abide anywhere where Buddha is to be found and where Buddha is not, he quickly passes.*

Samsara and Nirvana are a sole reality. This is why, for the awakened one, there is no distinction between the pure land of "Sukhavati-Paradise" and "Samsara", the cycle of birth and death. His multidimensional consciousness of all-embracing wholeness of being has risen above all discrimination between yes and no, and has transcended everything into the one truth. As the one who has awoken to the reality of the birth- and deathless mind, he has recognised the wonderful unity of life and death, and as such, the question of "to be or not to be" has lost its meaning for him.

> *Since he stops at neither of the two, even a thousand eyes cannot penetrate into his innermost essence.*

Lao-tse, the ancient Taoist master from the sixth century B.C. gives us in his Tao Te King, the book of Tao and effective force, an excellent description of an enlightened sage:

> The veritable masters of old
> were subtle, arcane and profound.
> Concealed they were, and inscrutable.
> Since inscrutable,
> I can describe them only with difficulty.

By dying into the Great Death, the awakened one has experienced his awakening from the dream of body, mind and world, and abides in the great affirmation and fullness of life. Since he has awakened to his birth- and deathless true self, he experiences himself as the one who has always been, but who now radiates as the self-mind. He experiences himself as unborn and undying and as eternity itself.

> When he has reached there,
> he encounters the mind of the old patriarchs
> of Zen.

When you reach this, you are in complete unison with all enlightened masters of the past, present and future. And whoever encounters you, equally encounters them all. That is why it is said in Zen, "Whoever sees a buddha, has equally seen all buddhas."

Having broken through the gateless barrier of great liberation, the ego-delusion has died the Great Death and there is nothing left of one's own darkness to be found. By realising non-discriminating clarity of mind, the enlightened one has reached a natural simplicity beyond wanting and rejecting and has surpassed all discrimination.

Since he is beyond the realm of discrimination, he has perfected the absolute negation of Zen and has completely transcended his consciousness in Enlightenment. In this great liberation of the mind, all notions of discrimination have fallen away so that no hint of holiness is to be seen in him. In his annotation to the poem, Kakuan says of this:

> *Even if a hundred birds would strew his path with wonderful flowers, this reverence would be completely meaningless to him.*

IX.

Having returned to the Origin

柳线牵风生远趣
艳华收

Poem and annotation by Kakuan

He has returned to the origin.
Yet his steps were in vain.
Better, were he from the beginning on
to have been as though blind and deaf –
dwelling in his true abode,
without longing for the external.
The river flows as it flows,
the red flowers are red of their own accord.

From the very beginning there is no dust – the truth is clear to see. He beholds the alternating coming and going of all life in the world and abides in serene non-action.
He does not allow himself to be deceived by the fleeting spectacles of this changing world. Why should he still trouble himself with anything at all?
The rivers flow blue, the mountains are green. He rests within himself and beholds the transformation of all things.

Comment by Zensho

He has returned to the origin.
Yet his steps were in vain.

The moment you awakened from the dream of body, mind and world, it was suddenly clear to you that your own mind is buddha and that from the beginning on, there was nothing to achieve.

When you have returned to the origin of your birth- and deathless true essence, you recognise that all your efforts were in vain. In fact, you had just taken on unnecessary hardship to find your true being, even though you had never really lost it since it was constantly present as the silent observer behind all experiences. Similarly, the Chinese Zen Master Pao-chi (ninth century) says:

> The Great Way cannot be achieved through practice. All talk of practice is just designed for ignorant people. When you have fathomed the principle and then look back at the practice, you will see for the first time that all your efforts were in vain.

You cannot find your true self through books and learning because it lies beyond all words and thinking. You can study all the sayings of the old masters, learn everything by heart, plus all the commentaries to go with them. Yet the instant you suddenly awaken to the radiating splendour of the One Mind, you will see that all of this was nothing more than chaff, of no further value.

Tokusan (ninth century), who later went on to become a tremendous Zen master, experienced this too. Tokusan was a great Buddhist scholar. He specialised in interpreting the Diamond Sutra and practised Zen under Zen Master Ryutan.

> Once evening he sat together with his master in the master's room. As it became dark the master said to Tokusan, "It is getting late, it is best if you go and sleep." Tokusan then took leave and went out. However, he quickly returned with the words, "It is very dark outside, I cannot see anything."
> Without saying a word, Zen Master Ryutan lit an oil lamp and handed it to him. As Tokusan reached out his hand to take the lamp, the master suddenly blew out the light in the lamp. In the same instant, Tokusan's mind shone ablaze and expanded into boundlessness, and he attained the Great Enlightenment.

The next morning, he took his entire collection of philosophical deliberations on the Diamond Sutra and burned them in front of the monastery while exclaiming, "Compared to the depths of the highest experience, all knowledge and learning is like a drop of water falling into the great abyss."

One day, as Tokusan was reading the Diamond Sutra, an inquisitive monk asked him which Sutra he was reading. Tokusan raised the Diamond Sutra up high and said, "This is the last to be burned."

The moment Enlightenment takes place, you recognise with radiating clear awareness that everything you had previously reached in your mental striving was just unnecessary ballast. Yet right from the start, had you been "as though blind and deaf" for all the scholarly, theoretical interpretations of the inexpressible truth, you could have spared yourself all the effort.

If you had immersed yourself in your innermost ground with your whole being from the beginning on, and had dissolved into it, your true essence as your "true abode" would have revealed itself in a flash. This is what the words of Zen Master Kakuan's poem for this ninth ox-herding picture tell us:

> Better, were he from the beginning on
> to have been as though blind and deaf –
> dwelling in his true abode,
> without longing for the external.

All your external seeking was nothing more than a pile of dust on the surface of the radiating mind-mirror, devoid of all reality. Since the mind is like a clear mirror, the reflections of discriminating thinking which cover reality are simply just like dust and dirt on the true mind. Yet when the erroneous thoughts vanish, the original mind appears of its own accord.

It is as though you would polish a mirror; when you have wiped away the dust, everything is transparent through and through, and beginningless, radiating clarity appears of its own accord. Kakuan says of this in his annotation to his poem:

> *From the very beginning there is no dust – the truth is clear to see.*

The Enlightenment experience is the great turning point in a person's life, which touches his whole personality. You experience a spiritual revolution, a tremendous "baptism by fire of the mind", which completely transforms your whole life. In this rebirth you have reached a new and entirely different state of being which radically changes your whole perspective and attitude to life.

> *He beholds the alternating coming and going of all life in the world and abides in serene non-action.*
> *He does not allow himself to be deceived by the fleeting spectacles of this changing world. Why should he still trouble himself with anything at all?*

However, abiding in serene non-action, "Wu-wei", does not mean passive inactivity. Instead, Wu-wei is a crystal-clear state of mind, out of which active participation is possible at any time, and the awakened one lets the universal effective force flow through him in his non-intervention.

It is harmonic accordance with the Tao, in which the awakened one abides in the all-fulfilling fullness of divine being. In this highest realisation of a multidimensional consciousness he lives in the all-embracing wholeness of being, in which he now experiences the whole universe as his own spiritual body – as his own absolute reality. The mind of the one who has thus returned to the original source becomes the source itself. Like the wind in the trees and the moon in the water, the completely liberated one lives in this enlightened consciousness of wonderful clarity. He lives his life in utter freedom and accordance with the entirety. The Zen masters and Taoists call this: "Flowing with the Tao".

Zen Master Mi-an (twelfth century) provides us with a very striking description of this wonderful state of mind: "When you have accomplished this, you are like a dragon above the clouds, like a tiger in the mountains. Everywhere, you are clear and calm. Everywhere, you are free to come and go as you please. Now you are able to rouse the wind and stir the grasses. You do not cling to any activity and you do not sit idly."

When the awakened one acts, he abides in so doing in non-action, and his deed is the wonderful deed of the buddhas. In the intentionless mind-state of cheerful-relaxed reflection of the mind, he observes the transformation of all things and beholds the alternating emergence and dissolution of all life in the world, without intervening.

> **The river flows as it flows,**
> **the red flowers are red of their own accord.**

From the moment onwards when the eye of wisdom opens for you in the instant of Enlightenment, you are in the "Sukhavati-Paradise" of boundless light. The Chinese Zen Master Yuan-wu from the twelfth century gives us a very striking description of this wonderful state of consciousness:

> Free of all boundaries; you have become open, light, and transparent. You gain the enlightened view into the true nature of all things, which now appear to you as a mass of glowing fairy-tale flowers without any tangible reality. This is where your naked, true self, the original countenance of your true being, reveals itself. This is where the wonderful landscape of your true native land lies unveiled before you, and you abide in the "Sukhavati-Paradise" of boundless light.

However, this paradise must not be viewed as a transcendental state of existence in space and time but as a pure consciousness dimension. For where is paradise to be found? Space is illusion – time is illusion. Thus, paradise can be nowhere other than exactly where you are "now-here".

As soon as you have recognised the universal voidness of everything, it all falls into place by itself and you spontaneously pervade all things. This voidness encompasses the whole universe and all beyond it, and contains all that exists within it as the all-fulfilling fullness of divine nothingness.

Reality reveals itself to you in all things. The sky, sun, moon, and stars, the mountains, trees and the rivers are a revelation of the all-fulfilling splendour of divine being. Everything is filled with the fullness of Tao and is the Tao itself. Therefore, the Chinese Zen Master Chih-chang (ninth century) calls out to us:

> Lo! A most auspicious light of great brightness shines in the entire cosmos. It makes everything visible at once – all countries, all oceans, all mountains, all suns and moons, all heavens and all worlds, each of which in a hundred thousand myriads. Oh monks, do you not then see the light?

The harmonic transformation of the Tao reveals itself in everything. It is the creative first principle from out of which all things are born, sustained and once again dissolved in never ending plenitude. He who has awakened to the radiating splendour of his true self lives in harmonic unison with the Tao, for in his realised consciousness, he has liberated himself for ever from the narrow perspective of a blinded, dualistic consciousness. The Chinese Zen Master Ma-tsu (eighth century) says this too:

> Following the essence is called being awakened, following phenomena is called being blinded. In the unenlightened state you are mistaken about your own consciousness. Being enlightened means recognising your own true essence.
>
> Once enlightened, you remain forever enlightened and you never fall back into the state of confusion. Just as once the sun has risen it does not unite with the darkness, once the radiating sun of wisdom has risen, there is never again a relapse into the apathy of spiritual blindness.

The great old masters of Zen point out again and again that the Enlightenment experience is possible for anyone who is truly prepared to completely let go of himself and all his familiar concepts. The Chinese Zen Master Shen-tsang (eighth century) describes this with the following words:

> Unparalleled, the wonderful light of your true self shines, indescribable in words and

letters. As soon as you just let go of your delusions, Buddhahood becomes reality.

By realising consummate multidimensional clarity of mind, the perfectly enlightened one has climbed above all discrimination. Both person and mind-ox have been completely transcended and he lives his life in the boundless freedom of being.

Since he has returned to the origin, he is no longer deceived by the fleeting phenomena of an external world of appearances. Likewise, he no longer requires any Zen practice as he is completely liberated from the cycle of birth and death. His sparkling-clear, enlightened self-awareness does not depend on any such exercise as sitting in immersion. In the words of Zen Master Ma-tsu, Zen thus says:

No practising and no sitting in immersion is the pure true Zen of all buddhas.

The consciousness of the awakened one who has achieved the birth- and deathless reality of his true essence is the realised self-mind. It is the self-mind which experiences the whole of creation as the self-revelation of the One Mind, beside which nothing else exists. In silent seclusion, he lives his oneness with the all-embracing wholeness of being and observes the natural motion of all things in cheerful-relaxed reflection of the mind.

> *The rivers flow blue, the mountains are green.*
> *He rests within himself and beholds the transformation of all things.*

Zen Master Mumon graces this mind-state of enlightened clarity of mind with a poetic verse:

> In spring, hundreds of flowers.
> In autumn, a full moon.
> In summer, a refreshing breeze.
> In winter, the snow.
> When you are in the enlightened clarity of the mind, every season is a good season.

X.

Entering the market with open hands

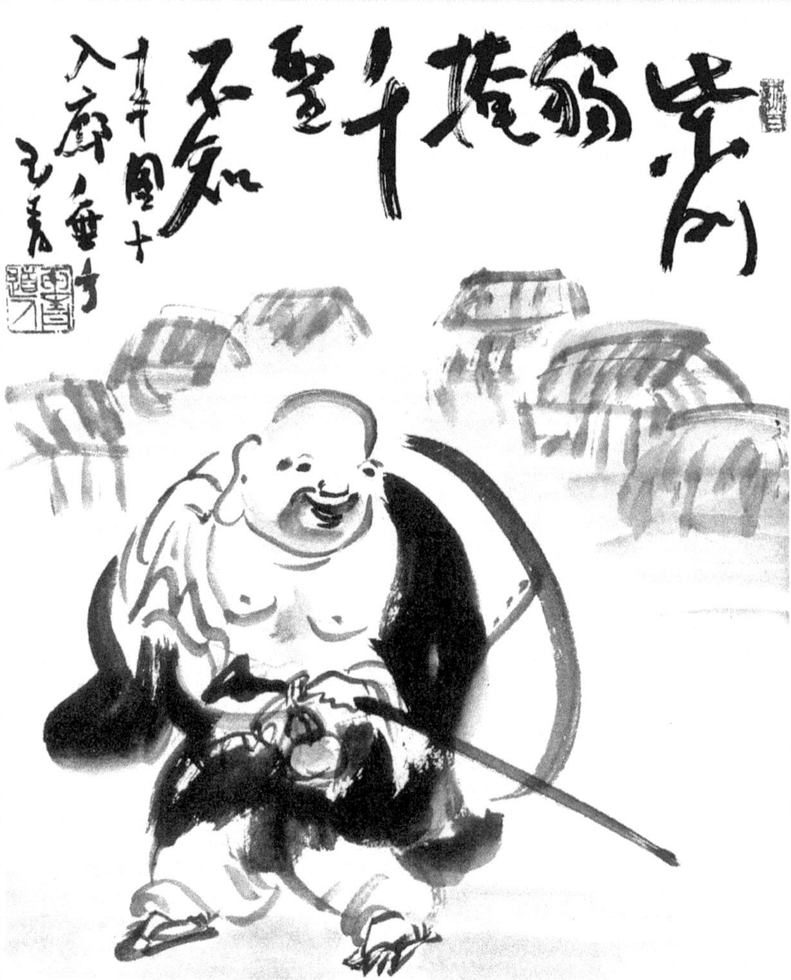
柴門獨掩千聖不知
十牛圖十
入鄽垂手

Poem and annotation by Kakuan

Bare chested and with naked feet,
he mingles with the people at the marketplace.
With ragged, dusty clothes,
his laugh covers his whole face.
Without performing miracles,
he causes withered trees to blossom.

Within his gates, even the wisest saints do not recognise him. The realm of the innermost is deeply concealed. He goes his own way – why should he follow the footprints of the patriarchs?
He enters the market with the gourd and returns to his hut with the walking staff. He shows bar-keepers and fishmongers the way to awakening to the true self.

Comment by Zensho

> Bare chested and with naked feet,
> he mingles with the people at the marketplace.

"Bare chested" means he returns to the world of everyday life with an open, giving heart. He is the fully awakened one, the liberated one, independent of everything; the one who has liberated himself from all distinction between Nirvana and the everyday world. For him, profane and sacred have become entirely one, for he now lives his life as the reality of the One Mind.

Nevertheless, a normal, dualistic consciousness cannot understand this all-uniting world experience of a free, perfectly enlightened and realised consciousness of non-discriminating wisdom. For how can be possible that, suddenly, the ordinary things of daily life are divine reality? How can the ordinary suddenly be the exceptional, and all of a sudden, pebble stones at the wayside become shining jewels?

Yet, the splendour of divine being is no unreachable, far-off, transcendental dimension, for it is now, here, right there where you currently are. The truth of Zen reveals itself this instant, right here. Immerse yourself completely in this instant! This the direct Zen way of instantaneously grasping reality, just as it is. For since absolute reality is the all-embracing wholeness of reality, it embraces boundless space and the three notions of time: past, present and future in a single "now". Here-now, everything falls together into one single point. In the words of the Tantra Master Saraha (ninth century):

> Everything that is here is everywhere and what is not here is nowhere.

When your eye of wisdom opens on experiencing the immediate presence of now through your awakening from the dream of birth and death, pebble stones truly become shining jewels. Then your whole being has transformed, for your consciousness is now that of the enlightened lucidity of the mind.

All the time, you experience nothing other than the world that matches your state of consciousness. For the world you experience is a reflection of your own projections. You create your own world. This means that when your consciousness is that of the dualistic perspective of spiritual blindness, you experience the dualistic world of grasping and rejecting. Then you live in a world of greed, hatred and blindness and you are trapped in your own projections. Zen Master Huang-po describes this situation with the following words:

> This pure Mind, the source of everything, shines forever and on all with the brilliance of its own perfection. But the people of the world do not awake to it, regarding only that which sees, hears, feels and knows as mind. Blinded by their own sight, hearing, feeling and knowing, they do not perceive the spiritual brilliance of the source substance.
> If they would finally throw off all conceptual thought in a flash, this source-substance would manifest itself like the sun ascending through the void and illuminating the whole universe without hindrance or bounds

Once you have awakened from the dream of birth and death, you abide in the enlightened world of all-embracing wholeness of being and experience everything as the One Mind, beside which nothing else exists. In this perfect realisation following the Enlightenment experience, whereby you rise above all discrimination, your entire world transforms into the revelation of transcendent wisdom. Now, you experience all worldly existence without exception as the timeless reality of the One Mind.

Zen Master Lin-chi gives us a good description of a realised sage: "He pervades the entire cosmos and moves freely and unimpeded in the world. Throughout the country, wherever he may go, he saves the beings." In the words of Lao-tse, the great old master of Taoism:

> The wise one does not have a closed heart,
> to him, the people's hearts are his own heart.
> The wise one lives quietly in the world,
> his heart is an open space.
> People see and hear him,
> and in all of them he sees his children.

By experiencing absolute oneness with all existence, he is likewise filled with all-encompassing compassion for all beings. Thus, in his unending mercy, he enters the everyday world.

> **With ragged, dusty clothes,**
> **his laugh covers his whole face.**

Since he is filled with the dynamic effective force of his inner experience of consubstantiality, he reaches out a rescuing hand to all people to liberate them from their subjugation to the cycle of birth and death and the suffering it brings with it.

The embodiment of this ideal of the enlightened one who turns to the world is known in Zen Buddhism as "Hotei, the laughing buddha". As a symbol of one who is perfectly liberated, he is seen as the incarnation of Maitreya, the buddha of all-encompassing love.

In Zen painting, Hotei is usually depicted as a small, bald, rotund man with a large sack slung over his shoulder and an infectiously broad smile covering his face. In Zen he represents the perfectly enlightened one who has broken through all boundaries and transcended the world. Hotei lives the free life of a Zen tramp, unattached and independent. Like the wind in the trees and the moon on the water he lived his life in total freedom and in accordance with the all-embracing wholeness of being.

He goes his own way – why should he follow the footprints of the patriarchs?

In his perfect realisation of Great Enlightenment, known in Zen as "Daigo-Tettei", Great Satori which reaches down to the deepest depths, the enlightened one has risen above any attachment to all of the patriarchs – to Buddha and all the other enlightened masters. Thus, just like them, he too has died the Great Death, "Dai-chi", and just as they have, he has awaked to the new, true life. So why should he then follow their footprints?

As the veritable enlightened one and thus perfectly liberated one, he himself has become a buddha and goes his own way, independent of everything.

He enters the market with the gourd and returns to his hut with the walking staff.

This "entering and returning" of the one who has awakened to his true being testifies to the great freedom of his actions, which emanate from his perfect realisation and unending mercy. Since he has risen above all discrimination between the profane external world and mystical introspection, everything has now become perfectly one for him. In the words of Zen Master Lin-chi: "Under way he is not far from his house. Distant from his house, he is not under way."

As the perfectly liberated one, he abides in absolute oneness with what is beyond the world, and is in harmonic unison with the requirements of the temporal world. He strides forth in the blazing light of the enlightened self-mind, in the midst of the changing world. His consciousness is the enlightened, scintillating state of the mind, in which only the immediacy of the present moment exists and nothing else. As the true person of Zen, he lives the truth of Zen through the realisation of interconnectedness and consubstantiality beyond all discrimination in the midst of the world. His awakened mind is completely free and he lives totally independently, and comes and goes as he pleases. He does this and that, but can equally leave it and do something completely different. He traverses the world of phenomena in utter freedom.

By immersing himself completely in what he does, he experiences the all-embracing wholeness of being in the midst of the world of phenomena. Each act of his daily life radiates in the light of the mind-ox.

Within his gates, even the wisest saints do not recognise him. The realm of the innermost is deeply concealed.

Even those considered also holy sages and as thousand eyes cannot penetrate his innermost realm. This would only be possible in an encounter with a fully enlightened being – someone on a par with him, a buddha. There is nothing special to be discerned in the awakened one's external appearance, so one cannot perceive anything holy or exceptional in him. Yet in his innermost ground of being he holds the shining jewel of the profoundest mystery as the gateway to all mysteries. For he experiences himself as the sole reality and the true basis of all creation and thus as the primary cause of all existence.

> *He shows bar-keepers and fishmongers the way to awakening to the true self.*

In his all-embracing consciousness – the unity of essence with all beings – he wanders thought the hustle and bustle of the world, serene and relaxed, in order to show the people the way to their lost mind-ox. For it has always been the highest concern of all truly enlightened masters to help the people experience their birth- and deathless true self. However, the way in which they lay bare the truth to the people varies greatly. The perfectly enlightened one, who Kakuan describes here in the tenth ox-herding picture, is the one who is completely liberated and who has risen above all rules and venerable norms of a religious consciousness.

In his realised consciousness of non-discriminating clarity, he makes no distinction between sacred and profane and thus a temple and a wine bar are equivalent for him. Wherever he may be, he abides in the boundless, all-fulfilling fullness of divine being.

Without performing miracles,
he causes withered trees to blossom

Without externally flaunting miracles he performs the greatest miracle of miracles by awakening the "spiritually dead" to life. As the perfectly liberated one he holds "the flame of non-discriminating wisdom" in the hand, with which he causes withered trees to blossom. In the language of Zen it is "the sword that kills and gives life".

A single stroke with the sharp sword of non-discriminating wisdom and all your delusions caused by dualistic, discriminating thought disappear. A single stroke and the bonds of your attachment to the interwoven memories of your dead past fall apart. One stroke and the endless vastness of the One Mind radiates forth. Zen Master Fo-yan (twelfth century) says of this:

> The power of non-thinking is like the embers of the all-consuming flame or the lightning-fast blow of a sharp sword. When the mind is free of thoughts, the lion's roar is reached. All further description would only place lesser minds in fear and confusion.

In the very powerful words of the Chinese Zen Master

Shih-tou (eighth century):

> Where the sword of wisdom flies, sun and moon lose their shine and heaven and earth lose their colour. Through this experience the devils' bellies burst and the eye of transcendental wisdom opens to you.

One single moment suffices, and everything is transformed in a spiritual explosion which shakes the world to its very foundations, and everything dissolves away. All experiencing of body, mind and world have gone. Only your true self remains, brightly shining in itself, without any object of perception. You experience your true countenance before your birth, the reality existing of itself, beside which nothing else exists. In an instant, your eye of Enlightenment opens, and for the first time, you see reality just as it is.

The small self has been completely destroyed in the Great Satori, the experience of essential voidness. It is the experience of the boundless vastness of the mind in which you experience your being and the entire cosmos as a single being.

The dark clouds of your spiritual blindness vanish in this great liberation from the chains of your self-created limitations. The mind radiates like the clear sky in boundless vastness and voidness, and nothing is able to darken it any longer.

Even when clouds cover the glowing moon, the moon is always there, just like the brightly radiating self-mind. It is constantly present, even when hidden behind the dark clouds of discriminating, conceptual thinking. To this, the following occurrence:

> The Chinese Zen Master Yun-chu from the ninth century said to a monk, "The self-mind is buddha." The monk replied, "Alas I cannot understand that. May I ask you to help me?" The master replied, "In order to help you, let us call the self-mind buddha. Turn your consciousness inwards and see yourself what this self-mind is."

The reality of our original, true essence lies within ourselves. There is nothing to reach and nothing to be changed. Our true self is already absolutely consummate and has always been so. In the radiating experience that the own mind is buddha and, as our original true essence, neither began with our birth nor will end with our death, the profound truth of Zen reveals itself to you.

Glossary

Adi-Buddha, Samantabhadra, Sanskrit, Original-buddha, absolute reality as the highest being in Tibetan-Buddhist cosmology. He is regarded as the personification of pure →Shunyata.

His →mantra is: OM AH HUM, which represents the body, speech and mind of all buddhas. Samantabhadra (Chin. Pu-hsien, Jap. Fugen), literally, "He of all-embracing kindness" is of great significance in Mahayana-Buddhism. He is seen as the embodiment of the equality of unity and diversity. He is the protector of all those who preach the dharma.

Amida Jap. for →Amitabha (Sanskrit)

Amitabha Sanskrit, "Boundless light", Jap. "Amida". One of the most important buddhas in →Mahayana Buddhism. It is the buddha of "western paradise" →Sukhavati, not linked to a particular location but instead, means a state of consciousness of boundless light, of love and comprehension.

Anitya Sanskrit, literally: "impermanence, fleetingness". In Buddhism, one of the three characteristics of all conditional arising and thus all being. Everything that has arisen, dwells for a while and then decays once again – it arises, exists and decays. Impermanence is the fundamental law of the whole of existence. The two other characteristics are derived from this: "Non-substantiality (Anatman)" and "Suffering (Duhkha)".

Avalokiteshvara Sanskrit, "the lord who looks down upon all things, or who hears the cries of the world". He is the →Bodhisattva of compassion and embodies all-encompassing compassion (→Karuna) with all suffering beings. His byname is "Mahakaruna", great mercy, one of the main facets of a buddha. The other main facet of a buddha is wisdom (→Prajna), which is embodied in a special way by Bodhisattva →Manjushri. Avalokiteshvara's boundless compassion is seen in his constant readiness to help all those beings who turn to him in their suffering. In Tibet, Avalokiteshvara is revered as Chenresi, in China as →Kuan-yin and in Japan as →Kannon (also Kwannon or Kanzeon).

Avatamsaka-Sutra Sanskrit →Hua-yen

Avidya Sanskrit, literally: "ignorance, non-recognising". Avidya is considered to be the root cause for the attachment to →samsara – the circle of birth and death. Ignorance is the root of all suffering, for it is that state of mind which is not in accordance with reality. In →Mahayana Buddhism, Avidya is denoted as non-recognition of the voidness (→Shunyata) of all things. Thus, non-recognition of the deceptive nature of all phenomena is the true reason for all suffering.

Bardo Tibetan, literally: "intermediate state", relates to the intermediate state between death and reincarnation. Buddhist teaching strongly stresses the direction-defining force of the state of mind of a dying person (meaning virtuous, not-virtuous or neutral) and also the negative influences of greed, hate and ignorance during bardo itself.

Beginner's mind →Shoshin

Bodhi Skt., literally: "Awakening, Enlightenment". →Satori

Bodhichitta Sanskrit, "Enlightenment-Mind", the endeavour to achieve Enlightenment for the good of all beings in order to free them from suffering. Also, the direct term for the enlightened Mind itself.

Bodhidharma, Sanskrit, (Jap. Daruma, Chin. Ta-mo). The 28th patriarch after →Buddha Shakyamuni in India and the first Chinese patriarch of →Zen. Since he came from India, which from a Chinese point of view is to the west, he was also known as "the barbarian from the West". Bodhidharma is a figure of Zen shrouded in mystery and very few details are known about him. He is the symbol of certain Zen-traits and the object of the often recurring question in the →Mondos: "What is the reason why Bodhidharma has come from the West?" The question means something like: What is the highest truth? What is my true essence?

Bodhisattva Skt., literally: "Enlightenment-being". A person who, having reached Enlightenment (→Satori), spends his life in the service of others to help them reach liberation. The term Bodhisattva is often used to denote a future →buddha.

Buddha Skt., literally: "the awakened one". 1. The historical Buddha Shakyamuni, who was born in India in ca. 563 B.C. 2. A person who has fulfilled complete Enlightenment (→satori), liberating him from the cycle of birth and death (→samsara). 3. The final truth, the true nature of all being.

Buddha-Dharma Sanskrit (Jap. Buppo), "buddha-law". The teachings of the historical Buddha Shakyamuni. In Zen however, we do not denote buddha-dharma as the teaching that can be conveyed in words, rather it is the highest truth, which is inaccessible for discriminating, conceptual thinking. It is that essential truth which led to Buddha's teachings and which can only be conceived in direct comprehension, in the experience of Enlightenment (→satori).

Buddha-Nature Skt., "Buddhata", the true nature of all beings, which makes it possible for a person to reach Enlightenment (→satori).

Chan Chin. for Zen (Jap.)

Cycle of birth and death →samsara

Daigo-Tettei Jap. literally: "Great →Satori, which reaches down to the ground". Highest complete Enlightenment. One of its principle characteristics is the experience of empty vastness and the lifting of all contrariety with the destruction of the small "I". Furthermore, the experience that the whole universe and the Self-Mind are completely identical.

Dharma Sanskrit, a term with various meanings. The teachings of →Buddha. Universal order and its laws. In this book, mainly used in the sense of the teachings of →Zen.

Dharmakaya Sanskrit, "Body of the great Order". The indescribable true being of the →buddhas, and at the same time, the essence of the universe.

Enlightenment →Satori

Enlightenment-Mind →Bodhichitta

Factor of existence →Skandha

Great Death →Satori

Hara Jap., literally: "Belly, abdomen". This common Zen term signifies the area approximately three finger widths below the belly button as the centre of all being. It is the centre of every person and at the same time the centre of the universe. Through the practice of →zazen and correct breathing a great energy and power develop in this centre. Hara, as the centre of energy, is in Zen the point of origin of all activity (as in the meaning of "acting on intuition", but in Zen its meaning goes much deeper).

Hinayana Sanskrit, "small vehicle". Oldest school of the two main branches of Buddhism. The original derogatory term "small vehicle" originates from the exponents of the later school of →Mahayana Buddhism. The main endeavour of Hinayana Buddhists is to reach their own liberation from →samsara, the cycle of birth and death. Here, little consideration is made for liberating other beings from the sea of suffering of samsara. In the rescue boot of the small vehicle there is only room for one person. Hinayana is viewed as the first step of Buddha's teachings. Only later did →Buddha reveal the complete teachings of Mahayana.

Hishiryo Jap., literally: "that which thinking cannot fathom". Zen term for →Enlightenment, which eludes all understanding through conceptual thought and thus transcends thinking.

Ho! Chin. This powerful, loud cry is often used by Zen masters as an abrupt means of expression to shatter the fixated, discriminating thinking of the student.

Hua-yen Chin., (Jap. Kegon, Skt. Avatamsaka), literally: "floral decorations" or "garland"; originally the name of a comprehensive →Mahayana text. The Hua-yen is seen by many Chinese and Japanese Buddhists as the crown of all Buddhist teachings and the perfection of Buddhist thought and realisation. Hua-yen is the doctrine of holistic being, and at the same time, a synthesis of all major Mahayana thinking. In Hua-yen, the universal One Mind is compared with the endless surface of the ocean, in which all things and events in mutual pervasion are an all-encompassing whole, which contains everything within itself. Everything is in perfect harmony together, for everything is the manifestation of the one principle – similar to the waves on the ocean. Everything in the universe, whether animate or not, is thus the One Mind, beside which nothing else exists.

Ishin-Denshin Jap., literally: "to transmit Mind by means of Mind". A fundamental concept of →Zen, often translated as "transmission of Heart-Mind to Heart-Mind". The term originates from the Platform Sutra by the sixth patriarch Hui-neng. In this →sutra, Hui-neng explains that the truth of Zen can only be realised through one's own experience, in a direct understanding of its true nature. Scholarliness gained through reading is worthless – thus Hui-neng's act of tearing apart the sutras. Zen Master Huang-po says: "There is no understanding through words, but merely a transmission from Mind to Mind."

Joriki Jap. The power of concentration gained through Zen meditation (→zazen).

Kannon, Kanzeon or also Kwannon, Jap. for →Bodhisattva →Avalokiteshvara.

Karma Sanskrit, literally: "Action or deed". The law of cause and effect, by which all thoughts and actions have a corresponding consequence. Through this we determine the quality of our own lives and influence that of others.

Karuna Sanskrit, literally: "compassion", all-embracing compassion. One of the two principal virtues in →Mahayana Buddhism; the other being →Prajna. (→Avalokiteshvara)

Kensho Jap., seeing one's own nature. →Satori

Koan Jap., literally: "public notice" (Chin. Kung-an). In Zen, the term for a paradox quote from a Zen master which points to the ultimate truth. A koan is there to aid a student of Zen in overcoming discriminating dualistic thinking so that he reaches the truth beyond all thinking. Koans play an important role in Zen instruction. A koan contains a question for which there is no answer for the intellect. To solve it, a higher intuition (→Prajna) is required. However, a koan is everything but a puzzle, since it requires the student to abandon his faith in his own, normal way of understanding. The answer lies beyond logic and it is there to aid the student to break through to the enlightened clarity of the Mind (→Satori).

The striking aspect of all koans is the alogicalness, the paradoxicalness of the words or the action. When one reads the answers of the old Zen masters to their students' questions, emanating from the Zen mind, one is confused and asks oneself what in fact the answer has to do with the question. It must be said here that these statements of the Zen masters have nothing to do with conceptual or intellectual ascertainments within our habitual limits of logical dualism. Instead we are dealing here with the manifestation of a tremendous experience of such all-encompassing universality that within it, all limitations of space and time and all language barriers are transcended.

Kuan-yin, Chin. for →Avalokiteshvara

Lin-chi-Tsung →Rinzai School

Mahayana Sanskrit, literally: "Great vehicle", as opposed to the earlier orthodox school of →"Hinayana". Mahayana Buddhism attaches a much greater importance to all-embracing compassion (Karuna) and the wish to help all beings reach liberation than it does to abstinence. Mahayana also includes the helping power of the →buddhas and →bodhisattvas.

Mahayana-Buddhism, Mahayana teachings →Mahayana

Maitreya Sanskrit (Jap. Miroku), literally: "The all-loving one". One of the five earthly →buddhas, the embodiment of all-embracing love. The Mahayana Buddhists anticipate that this, the last earthly buddha, currently abiding in Tusita Heaven, will come as a teacher of the worlds in around thirty thousand years' time.

Maitri Sanskrit, literally: "Goodness and mercy". One of the prime virtues in Buddhism. It is charitable goodness towards all beings, free from all attachments.

Maitri-Karuna literally: "Goodness and compassion". Fundamental state of mind of a →Bodhisattva, which is expressed in his desire to lead all beings to liberation.

Makyo Jap., approx. "devilish phenomena", deceptive, distracting phenomena and sensations which can arise during Zen meditation (→zazen). Makyos can appear in a variety of forms; as wonderful sounds, smells, faces, prophetic visions, sometimes also as levitation. However, Makyos are quite harmless as long as the zazen practitioner takes no heed of them and continues his practise unperturbed.

Manjushri Sanskrit (Jap. Monju), literally: "He who is noble and kindly". One of the most important → Bodhisattvas in →Mahayana Buddhism. Manjushri is the embodiment of wisdom. He is most commonly depicted with his sword of wisdom, cutting through ignorance. His raging Tantric appearance is that of the bull-headed Yamantaka, the vanquisher of death.

Mantra Sanskrit, one or a series of syllables, filled with spiritual energy, which the student recites either verbally or in the mind. Constantly repeating a mantra leads to realisation of the true being by way of purification of the thoughts. However, a mantra is only endowed with transforming powers when one has received it directly from the master (OM MANI PADME HUM).

Mara Sanskrit, Pali, literally: "Murderer, destroyer (of life)". Mara is the personification of the obstacles on the road to liberation. As the tempter and the phenomenon of unwholesomeness, he can be compared with the Christian devil, the "Father of lies". His three daughter are seen as his helpers: rait – desire, avati – discontent, and tanha – greed. In addition, Mara is supported by a whole army of demons.

Maya Sanskrit, literally: "Illusion, semblance, deception". In Vedanta philosophy (→Vedanta) Maya is the power of great illusion. It veils one's view so that one is unable to recognise Brahman, ultimate reality. Shankara links Maya to →Avidya, ignorance. Ignorance, that is, non-perception of the ultimate reality of Brahman, creates the delusion of an external world of phenomena in space and time by means of its obscurement. →Mahayana Buddhism characterises Maya as a deception or illusion, just like a phantasm created by a mirage. Individual things are provisory and have no existence of their own, they are in fact void (→ Shunyata) and mere conception.

Ming-Dynasty Chinese epoch from 1368 – 1644

Mondo Jap., "question-answer" (Chin. "Wen-ta"), a dialogue between Zen Master and student, also often just between Masters. In answer to a question concerning Buddhist truth or an existential problem, the student normally receives a paradox (→Koan), which cannot be classified by the intellect. The aim behind this is to smash the bounds of discriminating, conceptual thinking so that the student can obtain an answer from his innermost intuition (Heart-Mind).
A very well-known Mondo is: A Zen monk asked Zen Master Joshu: "What is the meaning of the first patriarch's coming from the west?" Joshu said: "The cypress tree in the courtyard."

Mu Jap. (Chin. Wu), literally: "Nothing, non-being, is not, has not, un-, none". One of the central concepts of →Zen and →Taoism. It describes utter freedom from all identification and attachment, and also stands for realisation of the void (→Shunyata). In the well-known Koan collection of the Mumonkan we encounter "Mu" in the first example, "Joshu's dog". In Zen it is also known as "the →koan Mu". "A monk respectfully asked Master Joshu: 'Does a dog have Buddha-Nature or not?' Joshu answered: 'Mu'".

Master Joshu's reply is simply "nothingness", which does not imply that a dog does not have →buddha-nature. Joshu knew just as well as the monk that all beings without exception have buddha-nature, and thus we must not misinterpret Joshu's MU as a negation.

His only intention was to prevent the monk from wanting to understand Zen through rational thinking. Instead, he should be striving towards that higher perception of reality, "beyond affirmation and negation", in which all contradictions melt away of their own accord.

The essence when dealing with a →koan is that the Zen practitioner achieve that crystal-clear state of consciousness, from which the words were spoken and which logical analysis can never reach. Only when the student's mind has sufficiently matured to the stage where it is completely congenial with the master's mind who gave him the koan, will the profound truth reveal itself which was hidden within the koan. (see also →koan).

Mumonkan Jap., literally: "The gateless gate". Alongside the →Pi-yen-lu, the most important collection of koans in Zen Buddhism (→Zen). It contains a collection of 48 →koans, compiled by Zen Master Mumon (thirteenth century) and accompanied by short Zen explanations.

Munen Jap. (Chin. Wu-nien); "Non-thinking, non-consciousness". Munen and →Mushin together form one of the central concepts of →Zen.

Mushin Jap., (Chin. Wu-hsin); "Non-thinking, non-consciousness, seclusion of the mind". A natural state of mind entirely without aim, beyond all thought.
Mushin and →Munen (Chin. Wu-nien) together form one of the central concepts of →Zen. In Zen, Munen does not mean ignorance or spiritual stupor but rather that the mind is so steadfast within itself that is cannot be perturbed by external circumstances, no matter what they may be.

Mushotoku Jap., "without aim and striving for gain."

Nembutsu Jap. (Chin. Nien-fo), invocation of the name of →buddha →Amitabha. The western meditation form of the Buddhist school of the Pure Land (→Pure Land School). The invocation recited is "Namu Amida Butsu" (Jap. for "homage to the buddha Amitabha"). Nembutsu recited in complete faith and absolute devotion leads to reincarnation in Sukhavati, the western paradise of the buddha Amitabha.

Nirvana Sanskrit, literally: "extinguishment". The state of complete liberation (→Enlightenment), as opposed to →samsara, imprisonment in the cycle of birth and death. The Zen Buddhist does not view nirvana as separate from the world but as a state of consciousness in which one fulfils one's true being and thus surpasses suffering.

Non-mind →Mushin

Pi-yen-lu Chin., literally: "Blue Cliff Record", Jap. Hekigan-roku. The most important collection of koans in Zen Buddhism (→Zen) alongside the →Mumonkan. It was published in the twelfth century by the Chinese Zen Master Yuan-wu, one of the most significant masters in the history of Zen. It involves a collection of 100 →koans which, together with additional texts, belong to the zenith of the whole of Zen literature.

Prajna Sanskrit, literally: "Wisdom" (Pali: Panna, Jap. Hannya). In →Mahayana Buddhism Prajna is intuitively experienced insight into the voidness (→Shunyata) of all phenomena. Prajna is one of the principle characteristics of Buddhahood.

Pratitya-Samutpada Sanskrit, literally: "Emergence in mutual conditionality and dependence". The doctrine of the chain of conditional emergence is the foundation of all Buddhist schools. A deeper understanding of Buddhism depends on one's grasp of this doctrine. The Pratitya-Samutpada shows that all phenomena have no more than an empirical validity and are thus devoid of reality. All phenomena exist respectively in a causal and conditional relationship of dependence on each other and to each other. Nothing is to be found which is non-dependant and which has an existence out of itself.

Pure Land (Chin. Ching-tu, Jap. Jodo) →Sukhavati

Pure Land School →Amitabha

Rinzai School (Chin. Lin-chi-tsung, Jap. Rinzai-shu). Alongside the →Soto school, one of the predominant schools of Zen Buddhism (→Zen) in Japan. The striking feature of Rinzai is the systematic use of →koans for gaining Enlightenment (→Satori).

Samadhi Sanskrit (Jap. Sanmai or Zanmai), literally: "to fasten, to fix". A state of non-intentionality and freedom from thoughts. It is the state of focussing on a single object, brought about by calming the activity of the mind. In this non-dualistic state of consciousness the person meditating and the object of meditation become completely one. All dualism and the belief in a self, existing of itself and separate from everything else are overcome in Samadhi. However, this state of consciousness of Samadhi, free of all thinking, is neither stuporous nor unfeeling. Quite the contrary, it is the crystal-clear awareness of the Mind. A person immersed in Samadhi experiences an intensive feeling of inspiritment of a psychic-physical nature, which is immeasurably greater than everything that he has previously experienced.

Samantabhadra →Adi-Buddha

Samsara Sanskrit, literally: "roaming". The cycle of birth and death. The aim of all Buddhists and Hinduists is liberation from samsara, and thus from suffering. It is liberation from the imprisonment in the wheel of – birth, ageing, despair, illness, pain and death.

Satori Jap. (Chin. Wu). Zen term for the experience of Enlightenment, or awakening. Satori is far more than an intuitive understanding of true being, as in the experience of →Kensho, since the person who experiences Satori dissolves entirely into it. In →Zen, Satori is described as the rebirth of the true self once the false, illusory self; the ego-delusion has died the "Great Death".

Sesshin Jap., literally: "Concentration of the Heart-Mind". Intensive →zazen sitting periods lasting several days in total, interspersed with speeches by the master and the opportunity of a one-to-one talk (Dokusan).

Shastra Sanskrit, literally "textbook, instruction".

Shikantaza Jap., "Just sitting". →Soto school

Shoshin Jap., "Beginner's mind". The necessary state of mind of a Zen student for Zen instruction by a master. It is the attitude of mind in which the student recognises that he knows nothing. It is the absolute prerequisite for letting go of everything that sense and reason can comprehend.

Shunyata Sanskrit (Jap. Ku), literally: "emptiness, void". According to the teachings of Mahayana nothing possesses a self-dependent, lasting substance. All things are empty and thus without self-nature. The teaching of shunyata is one of the cornerstones of the whole of →Mahayana Buddhism and accordingly of →Zen. It is very subtle and cannot be expressed in words. Although there is extensive literature covering this subject, shunyata is only completely understandable for those who have experienced it themselves it in the experience of Enlightenment (→Satori).

Skandha Sanskrit (Pali: Khandha), "group, amassment". In Buddhism, the five groups which constitute and define the human personality as it is commonly known.

Corporeality group (Rupa)

Sensation group (Vedana)

Perception group (Samjna)

Mental formations, psychic forming force (Samakara)

Consciousness (Vijnana)

What we commonly view as being our personality is in truth nothing more than a mere process of these psychic-physical phenomena, which means that it is no more than a sum of nonpersonal factors of existence.

Soto School (Chin. Tsao-tung-tsung, Jap. Soto-shu). Alongside the →Rinzai school, one of the two principle schools of Zen Buddhism (→Zen) in Japan. As opposed to Rinzai, Soto does not make use of →koans but rather, it practises a form of Zen comprised exclusively of just-sitting →Shikantaza, literally: "nothing but sitting". Since it insists on putting zazen on a par with Enlightenment (→Satori), Soto is known as "silent

Enlightenment Zen".

Sukhavati Sanskrit, "blissful", the western paradise, ruled by →buddha →Amitabha. Reincarnation in Sukhavati paradise has the effect that one can no longer fall back into a reincarnation in another area (→Nembutsu).

Sung-Dynasty Chinese epoch, 960-1278

Sutra Sanskrit, literally "guideline". Sutras are the most important texts in Buddhism. Most of the sutras are instructive talks by →Buddha. In →Mahayana Buddhism many additional sutras were later written and are regarded as being authoritative. They emerged between the first century B.C. and the sixth century A.D.

Tang-Dynasty Chinese epoch, 618-906; the period in which Zen Buddhism was at its peak (→Zen).

Tao Chin., literally: "Way", central metaphysical term of →Taoism. Tao is the Absolute, the fundamental all-encompassing principle; the ultimate truth. Tao forms the core of Lao-tse's

→ Tao Te King and the teachings of Chuang-tse. The aim of all Taoists is to live in unison with Tao. Intellectual understanding is not enough, instead it is a matter of fulfilling the unity, simplicity and →voidness of Tao. "Action without intent", →Wu-wei, literally: Non-action, is seen as the principal attitude of mind of a Taoist.

Taoism There are two main streams of Taoism – the philosophical stream: Tao-chia, and the religious stream: Tao-chiao. Tao-chia dates back to the Taoist master Lao-tse and his book, the →Tao Te King. Here, acting without intent in unison with →Tao is seen as the highest ideal. On the other hand, the aim of the religious Taoism is physical immortality. It is to be achieved through breathing exercises, physical exercises and certain sexual practices.

Tao Te King Chin., literally: "The book of Tao and true virtue". A work from the sixth century B.C. ascribed to the old Taoist master Lao-tse. The Tao Te King is the cornerstone of →Taoism and at the same time one of the most important and most translated books of world literature.

Tathata Sanskrit, "Thusness, thus-being, that which is." A core concept of →Mahayana Buddhism. It describes the Absolute, the true nature of all things. Tathata is beyond all dualistic concepts, it is unchanging and the opposite of all apparent phenomena. As the thusness of all things it is formless, uncreated and without self-nature. It is identical to →buddha-nature and thus equivalent to the →dharmakaya.

Tathagata Sanskrit, literally "The one who has thus gone (thus arrived there, thus come)". This term is used as an honorary title to express Buddha's identity as a consummate being. As a perfectly enlightened →buddha he acts as a mediator between the Absolute and the world of phenomena.

Te Chin., literally: "virtue, power". The spiritual force of the →Tao, as revealed to those who live in unison with the Tao. Lao-Tse calls "Te", true virtue in his Tao Te King. It is what can be called spontaneous experience through Tao.

Vedanta Sanskrit Advaita-Vedanta

Void, emptiness →Shunyata

Wu Chin., literally: "Nothing, non-being". → Mu

Wu-hsin Chin. →Mushin

Wu-nien, Chin. →Munen

Wu-wei Chin., literally: "Non-action" in the sense of "action without acting". This Taoist term is not to be confused with passively doing nothing. Much rather, it means the attitude of mind of non-intervention in the natural course of things. In truth, Wu-wei is a highly effective state of mind, in which any action is possible at any time. By living non-action, the Taoist sage is in unison with Tao, whose universal power is brought to bear exactly due to this non-action. The great Taoist master of old, Lao-tse thus says in his →Tao Te King:
Tao is eternally without action, but nothing remains undone. Wu-Wei is therefore a matter of creative non-action, an actless conduct which underlies the mental attitude of non-intervention and the courage of letting things happen. Wu-Wei transcends both extremes – restless activity

and absolute inactivity. It is a non-action of the unimportant, which at the same time allows the essential to take effect.

Yamantaka Sanskrit →Manjushri

Zanmai Jap. →Samadhi

Zazen Jap. (Chin. Tsao-chan), literally: "sitting in immersion", the common meditation practice in →Zen. All great masters of Zen view zazen as a practice which is indispensable and fundamental in Zen. Zazen is abiding of the Mind in a state of crystal-clear awareness, free of content and not focussed on any object.

Zen Jap., an abbreviation of "Zenna", the Japanese way of reading the Chinese "channa" (in short, "chan"), which itself is a transcript of the Sanskrit word "Dhyana. Zen-Buddhism developed in the 6th and 7th centuries in China from the combination of Bodhidarma's transmission of Indian Dhyana-Buddhism and Chinese Taoism. Characteristic of Zen is its particularly strong emphasis on the experience of Enlightenment

(→Satori). Integral to Zen is also the development of intuitive comprehension through meditation (→zazen) instead of intellectual studies.

In the ninth century the Chinese Zen masters developed a new teaching method. From then on, the masters made use of paradoxical phrases (→koans) in order for their students to gain an understanding of the truth beyond discriminating, conceptual thinking. Here, they often employed violent methods, such as hitting, kicking or shouting to open the eye of Enlightenment of their students. From the 12th century onwards the Zen masters called on their students to concentrate on a koan for so long until they reached Enlightenment.

Contact

ZEN-ZENTRUM
TAO CHAN

Tao Chan Zentrum e.V.
Gemeinnütziger Verein
Adelheidstrasse 37,
65185 Wiesbaden
Germany

The Tao-Chan Zen Centre is under the personal direction of Zen Master Zensho W. Kopp.
During his many years as an active spiritual master, a large community of students have come together whom he regularly instructs.

Zen-Day

Twice a month, the Tao-Chan Zen Centre organises an open Zen-day, led by Zen Master Zensho W. Kopp.

Information and registration
Tel. +49 (0)611 940 623-1 Fax -2
www.tao-chan.org
www.facebook.com/ZenZentrumTaoChan

Books by Zen Master Zensho W. Kopp

All books available at: www.tao-chan.org

The power of inner quietude
Turn the light of spiritual awareness back to the inner source of your true essence, which is pure joy and bliss.

ISBN 978-3-752670-55-4

Living in inner fullness
Aphorisms of a Western Zen Master

ISBN 978-3-751935-09-8

Modern ZEN-ART
Watercolours and sayings of a Western Zen Master

ISBN 978-3-907246-09-2

DE /EN

Enlightened Dimensions of the Divine
Paintings and quotations of a Western Zen Master

ISBN 978-1-4827-9942-2

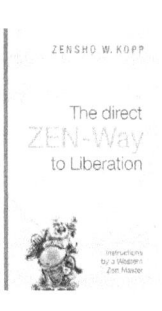

The direct ZEN-Way to Liberation

A profound wisdom which transforms and liberates

ISBN 978-3-752641-15-8

Awakening to Your True Self
The Zen way of all-embracing mysticism

ISBN 978-3-751931-82-3

True Life Through Zen
Spiritual self-realisation in daily life

ISBN 978-3-734743-55-9

Words of the Awakened Mind
Aphorisms of a Western Zen Master

ISBN 978-3-848241-34-7

The Freedoom of Zen
The Zen book that shatters all limits and bounds

ISBN 978-3751937-01-6

Lao-tse – Tao Te King
The Book of Tao and Spiritual Force

Transcription by Zen Master Zensho W. Kopp

ISBN 978-3-842328-61-7

Audio Books

Awakening to your True Self

ASIN B08CWM84W1

Lao-Tse Tao Te King

2 Cds

ASIN B00DTX9RJK

Music CDs

Satori

The Great Liberation

ASIN: 887936949722

Transformation

Mystical Sound Dimensions

ASIN: B00H4H0NVS

Lightning Source UK Ltd.
Milton Keynes UK
UKHW021139020223
416362UK00015B/1013